FRESH M

To Max!

The best of everything always,

Jon

2015

FRESH MUSIC

EXPLORATIONS WITH THE CREATIVE WORKSHOP ENSEMBLE

FOR MUSICIANS, ARTISTS, AND TEACHERS

JON DAMIAN

YO! Publications, Cambridge, MA

Fresh Music: Explorations with the Creative Workshop Ensemble for Musicians, Artists, and Teachers
YO!Publications

ISBN 978-0-9863105-0-8

Library of Congress Control Number 2015901154

Editing: Betsy Damian, Evelyn Rosenthal

Cover design: Jon Damian
Book design: Wm.R.Brinkley & Associates. Inc.
Printed in the United States of America

p. 139: Excerpt from "Mommy, What's a Rubbertellie"? © 2007 by Jon Damian.
p. 152: "La Danza della Scarpetta: A Perugian Recipe" by Jon Damian '74 appeared in *Berklee Today*, 22, no. 1 (Fall 2010); published by permission.

Fresh Music: Explorations with the Creative Workshop Ensemble for Musicians, Artists, and Teachers is based on true events and real characters.
Some character names have been changed to create a sense of story.
It is a composite work of creative nonfiction.

Front cover: Author Jon Damian in lecture performing "Rubbertellie Murals" in Melbourne, Australia, at the Northern Melbourne Institute of TAFE(NMIT). "Rubbertellie Murals" is a multimedia piece, and is part of a larger work, *By-Produx*, composed by Jon. He states: "In the *By-Produx* series of works, I show that all media exist at the same time. Exciting sound art exists in the brush sounds of the painter. The cover depicts my fingers playing and painting on the strings of my Rubbertellie as a 20-foot length of paper moves along, seismographically producing a mural and a sound sculpture simultaneously." Photo by Phil Spicer.

Back cover: The author performing "Rubbertellie Murals" at the Northern Melbourne Institute of TAFE(NMIT). Photo by Phil Spicer.

email: jdamian@berklee.edu
website: jondamian.com

CONTENTS

FOREWORD

I decided to use this letter from John D'Auria, principal of the Wellesley Middle School, for the foreword of *Fresh Music: Explorations with the Creative Workshop Ensemble for Musicians, Artists, and Teachers*. The letter captures beautifully the philosophy of the Creative Workshop Ensemble, and I thank Principal D'Auria for kindly giving me permission to use it.

—Jon Damian

Dear Parents,

A few weeks ago I had the opportunity to observe our guest artist, Jon Damian, work with the members of our Jazz Band. Damian is a professional musician, author of *The Guitarist's Guide to Composing and Improvising*, and a professor at Berklee College of Music. In this 45-minute class, his goal was to have students listen carefully to one another's musical expressions, and based on what they heard, respond in an improvisational manner. His overarching aim was to have students "play in the moment."

Watching this class unfold was fascinating. Damian had to first peel back habits students had developed during their musical training. There were no specific notes to play, and the direction for this composition was not coming solely from a conductor. Instead, students heard about a context ("This piece is about a coronation of a King and Queen. Think of yourselves as villagers invited to a huge party."). Students were given some direction about rhythm, timing, and a scale to use as a basis for their music creations. Slowly, and with some hesitation, students began to venture out and play in response to both the context and what they heard from one another. By the end of the period, a musical piece emerged that fit the context, including an aria by a King followed by a reply from the Queen while "villagers" played segments that appropriately accompanied the coronation of these royal figures. The students had clearly started to "play in the moment."

Observing this group of talented musicians struggle with the creative process, especially with the idea of relying more on their own senses rather than written music, led me to wonder if we provide enough opportunity in school to practice what Robert J. Sternberg, who directs the Center for the Psychology of Abilities, Competencies, and Expertise, calls the "creativity habit." According to Sternberg, while it may sound paradoxical that creativity is a habit or a routine response, his research indicates that creative people are "creative not by any particular inborn trait, but because of an attitude toward their work, and even toward life: They habitually respond to problems with fresh and novel approaches rather than allowing themselves to respond in conventional, and sometimes automatic ways."[1] Sternberg also suggests that like any habit, creativity can either be encouraged or discouraged.

Sternberg raises the question of whether or not the increase in conventional standardized testing that has emerged to provide educational accountability has unintentionally suppressed creativity. Conventional standardized tests, according to Sternberg, encourage a certain kind of learning and thinking—"the kind of learning and thinking for which there is a right answer and many wrong answers." Divergent thinking is not one of the values we currently support with MCAS.[2]

Is creativity important? Is it something that we should value in our teaching and our assessments? The fast pace of change that characterizes modern day life and the unforeseen challenges, problems, and obstacles that frequently come our way often require a nimble cognitive response. Rarely, in my experience, do the problems that we or our children face have solutions that emerge from the simple application of a formula. Most problems are ill structured and require a blend of knowledge, insight, intuition, and creativity to solve.

When is it too early to start practicing creativity? Some might argue that creativity emerges only after a knowledge base is mastered and thus should be practiced at a later point in schooling—college or graduate school. If, as Sternberg's research suggests, however, creativity is a way of thinking, the longer we wait in school to practice it, the less likely it will become a habit of mind.

As I unpack twenty large boxes of MCAS tests that now sit in my office awaiting distribution and as I review how much time we now expend on standardized testing compared to a decade ago, I can't help but wonder whether "improvisation" will be known better as an SAT vocabulary word rather than as an important way of thinking and as a vital way to solve the problems that we encounter outside the confines of a test.

John D'Auria

Principal
Wellesley Middle School

---

1. Robert J. Sternberg, "Creativity Is a Habit," *Education Week*, February 22, 2006.
2. MCAS is the standardized testing program in Massachusetts public schools.

ACKNOWLEDGMENTS

Thanks to my wife Betsy for her loving and tireless support, and her editing, and to my wonderful children, Ben and Tara, and Isabel Rose, and Gene and Monique-Adelle.

Thank you to my early creative music workshop friends and teachers, John Voigt, Bill Elgart, Tom Plsek, and Dr. Mark Harvey.

Thank you to all the Creative Workshop participants for their support and their creative ideas, from which I will always draw inspiration, and especially to: Nico Alzetta, Chris Bartos, Joey Bennett, Andy Berman, John Bishop, Joe Cohn, Thomas Dowd, Guillaume Estace, Craig Ferguson, Bill Frisell, Michael Geiler, Josh Gerowitz, Dan Gianaris, Francesco Guaiana, Corey Hendricks, Andrew Hock, Eric Jensen, Sten Höstfält, Yuto Kanazawa, Wayne Krantz, Graham Lambert, David Lee, Jonathan Lipscomb, Blaze McKenzie, Robert Mulyarahardja, Mastaneh Nazarian, Braydon Nelson, Shu Odumura, David Ostberg, Ezra Platt, Andre Poinciano, John Remington, Pavel Rivera, Kurt Rosenwinkel, Az Bin Abd Samad, Cole Shuster, Austin Smith, Niccolo Soffiato, Adam Tressler, Ville Vokkolainen, James Wilkie, Daniel Wright, and Stash Wyslouch.

Thank you to Larry Baione and the Berklee College of Music for supporting the workshop by including it in the college's curriculum. Thanks to Gene Damian for a quote, and his artwork; to Monique-Adelle Callahan for poetry inspiration; to Fred Bouchard for Messiaen support, and editorial assistance; to Ezra Platt for his "Tone Maze" idea; to Judson Crane for "The Alphabet Tune"; to Henry Platt and his wonderful Wellesley bands; to Shintaro Hanada for haiku; to John Bisbee for photo permission; to Takaya Ono for his "Wonder Wheel" idea; to Phil Spicer for the cover photos; to Dave Miranda for his pasta illustration; to Mark Small for his *Berklee Today* support; to Ruthie Ristich for graphic advice; to Evelyn Rosenthal for editing; to William Brinkley for book design; to Julie Campbell for technical support; to Rob Hayes and Tom Riley for information support; to Ralph Rosen, Jimmy Kachulis, Rich Appleman, and John Wilkins for gossip support; to Roger Dell for art research; to Alex Pinter for blinking technique; to Christine Hoggatt for editorial assistance; to Larry Monroe, Giovanni Tomasso, and Greg Badolato for supporting the Creative Workshop on the road; to David Goodrich for dpi research; to Carolyn Wilkins for mystery research; to Stephane Wrembel for his words of support; to Tim Wolf for his BluesShape pizza; to Jackson Fitzgerald for his "Beautiful" idea; to Rob Lee for his cyber wisdom; and to everyone else who offered generous help along the way.

INTRODUCTION

When one tugs at a single thing in nature he finds it attached to the rest of the world.
—John Muir

ORIENTATION MEETING

On one level, this is a book about musical improvisation. On another, it is about creativity in general. Whatever your art form—music, writing, teaching, dance, acting, sculpture, drawing, painting, ceramics, architecture, cooking, public speaking, landscaping, or simply living well (for a life can be a work of art)—it is my hope that you will find ideas here that will serve as catalysts for your creative endeavors. Some of the techniques in this book are my own, but many I have shamelessly stolen from other creative artists, for that's what artists do: they borrow, combine, recombine, juxtapose, and react against the works and methods of others. Out of this creative engagement, magic happens.

According to the ancient Greeks, on Mt. Parnassus there was a spring sacred to the Muses. Drink from this spring and creativity would course through your body and spirit. Great story, but there is no single wellspring of creativity. There is, however, one characteristic that all people have in common in their creative moments: something Buddhists call mindfulness— really being there, and being receptive.

During my years as a performer, teacher, and student of improvisation, I have noticed that the more technically advanced we become as improvisers, the less we tend to respond to the moment. The above quotation from the great naturalist John Muir is an appropriate opening for this book because when a person is really attentive to the moment, he or she doesn't just see but fully experiences unexpected connections. To explore ways to make my students—as well as myself—receptive to creative moments, I founded the Creative Workshop Ensemble at the Berklee College of Music in Boston.

Fresh Music chronicles the Creative Workshop Ensemble's beginnings, a fun, creative time in my life. The earliest creative workshop ensembles I co-led were the Rubbertellie String Quartet and the Boston New Music Ensemble in the 1970s. I've written this book to share with musicians, artists, and teachers what I have learned from leading and playing with some of the greatest creative musicians.

As workshop members, we should think of ourselves as polyartists—artists in all media. In the Creative Workshop Ensemble simple organic concepts and language are used (up, down, a lot, a little), easily translatable to various artistic media. As polyartists, and as Homo sapiens, we share a common, mutual medium, our being. Through our chosen artistic medium we share our essential selves with others. For me, this sharing is the true beauty of the arts. Using only the inherited language of some particular academic medium—that is, just following the rules—will cause you to produce pulseless, clonelike, incestuous, generic art. Rich, unique, organic, effortless art is grown by individuals interacting with the universe we live in, by people who have developed their ability to be receptive and to be creatively inspired by the amazing stuff that happens in the moment, and by the rules as well. This book will help you to prepare for and set up such creative moments. What Louis Pasteur said of scientific discovery applies to artistic discovery as well: "Chance favors the prepared mind." Much of what is in this book I have learned from my students and colleagues. I anticipate receiving wonderful reflections from you, to continue this creative conversation.

Participants in the Creative Workshop Ensemble, affectionately called "CreW," don't need advanced technical music skills, and you will not need them either, dear reader. I therefore welcome you as a full-fledged workshop member. Glad you could join us. The goal of this workshop is to help you to heighten communication and observation skills, and to truly create in the moment—to compose and improvise original works of art spontaneously. Inspirational sources for workshop compositions range from the alphabet to the zodiac, from Bach to bop, and from jelly beans to doughnuts. For one piece, we even had a goldfish serve as conductor! Guest artists from various media, including dance, drama, and the visual arts, have visited the workshop and developed workshop concepts through their particular art form. We even had a visit by a clown. I invite artists in all media to participate in and expand on workshop activities and concepts.

CreW members develop their musical communication skills by exploring the basic sound dimensions: dynamics (loudness, softness), rhythm (activity, inactivity), direction (up, down), and articulation (sharp, smooth). These dimensions of sound are analogues of (and help to produce) the spatial dimensions of depth (dynamics), width (rhythm), height (direction), and contour (articulation). In other words, they translate into the visual arena, and are profoundly connected to all the visual and performance arts, including the most sacred one, teaching. In every situation, a greater awareness of these dimensions strengthens creative potential and awareness of essential forms. Workshop participants quickly learn that true creative improvisation is the ability to be aware of a moment and to react to it efficiently. This is the first of many statements that apply to creative work in all artistic media that you will encounter in this book.

My work as a professional illustrator before becoming a professional musician and music professor helps me to see, and hear, the unbroken connections between artistic media— the dance in a musician's body as she performs; the lovely rhythmic music sounding from a dancer's feet interacting with the floor; the visual dance and percussive sounds of a sculptor's hammer, chisel, and stone; the cascade of images as a scene takes form in the mind of a writer; and so on.

Fresh Music: Explorations with the Creative Workshop Ensemble for Musicians, Artists, and Teachers offers an invitation to join in creative explorations. The book's activities will inspire new creative musings. This is a "how would you" book, not a "how to" book.

The ideas presented in this book are truly workshop-inspired. The Creative Workshop Ensemble at its best is a creative community, holistically at work, building exciting art in the moment, and with integrity. I am constantly tapping into and enjoying the innate creative genius of each workshop member, including myself. You, as a reader, are now a workshop member.

Please contact me with your own ideas, inspired by workshop concepts, in any medium you wish. May I quote the author Jamie Magee:

The end is not the reward; the path you take is the reward.

Writing this book, and being a part of the Creative Workshop Ensemble, is an exciting path for me, and I hope it opens up exciting new paths for you.

How to Use This Book

AS A TEACHER AND WORKSHOP DIRECTOR

Fresh Music explores a semester of the Creative Workshop Ensemble—fourteen weeks of activities. Use the book as a syllabus, moving week to week, or stimulate and/or create your own course or workshop syllabus for a group of any idiomatic persuasion, and in any artistic medium. In *Fresh Music* the concepts and ideas presented are applicable to grades K through college, and in any setting from private instruction to full ensemble. Let the roles of teacher and student become one. A workshop, a classroom, is a living, breathing creative medium for imaginations.

AS A PERFORMER

Join in to play, dance, and act with the workshop. Be fearless, and have fun. CreW's concepts create an atmosphere of no idiomatic shoulds or coulds, a guilt-free environment. Use this improvisatory freedom to find your special music, your special dance.

AS A COMPOSER, WRITER, AND CHOREOGRAPHER

In the Creative Workshop, the entire world is the stimulus for our creative ideas. Any archetype can work as an inspiration for workshop compositions. Let CreW's holistic attitudes inspire your work and expand your writing resources.

AS AN ENSEMBLE LEADER

Use the themes throughout the book as catalysts for your ensemble's creative work and to build communication abilities and an ongoing exchange of ideas. Stimulate a workshop consciousness in your ensemble.

AS A MUSIC AND ART THERAPIST

Build confidence in your group through the creation and execution of workshop ideas. The Creative Workshop has been therapeutic for many workshop participants. As saxophonist Albert Ayler titled his classic recording, "Music Is the Healing Force of the Universe."

AS A CREATIVE ARTIST IN ALL MEDIA

Throughout *Fresh Music* you will find suggestions for applying insights from the Creative Workshop to work in other media, but the best insights will be yours—the ones you come up with. Think of my suggestions simply as a glimpse at possibilities.

I tell the workshop that as artists, the true joy and reward are received in the actual production and performance of concepts and ideas, in the moment. The ideas presented in this book are meant to be works in progress, infinitely changing in interpretation (for such is one of the joys of improvisation), and are meant to be used merely as springboards for your own inventions in your artistic medium.

Take the ideas and concepts presented here into your lives. Enjoy their moments. May they give you a view into your own infinity of possibilities and increase your engagement with, and enjoyment of, this wonderful world.

Fresh Music chronicles an actual workshop situation with dialogue between me and the other workshop members. Since you are now a workshop member, there is direct dialogue between me and you, my dear reader and fellow artist, as I often pull you aside to share ideas with you.

There is an unbroken connection between all art media. Send me your works, your ideas, your questions. I look forward to continuing this conversation beyond these pages.

CHAPTER 1 – WEEK 1
COMMUNICATION 101

The real voyage of discovery consists not in seeking new landscapes but in having new eyes [and ears].
—Marcel Proust

I am standing at the whiteboard, sketching my name, and contact information for the soon-to-be-arriving spring semester class of the Creative Workshop Ensemble. As I write, I am impressed by the magic of written language—its power to communicate—and I realize that communication will be the central, overarching theme to all the workshop's activities through the upcoming semester. The workshop's success depends on effective communication, most importantly starting with today's class.

Ezra, the first arrival, greets my back as I stand at the board.

EZRA: Good morning, Jon!

JON: Nice to see you!

For the past year, Ezra has been a private studies student with me, and is excited to be a part of the workshop since hearing stories from his father, a former student of mine, about the workshop's early beginnings. As I finish at the board, more students silently arrive, and a quorum is achieved. I greet the class.

JON: Welcome to the Creative Workshop Ensemble. We as workshop members affectionately, and acronymically, refer to ourselves as "CreW." You follow in a long line of distinguished participants.

I direct the class's attention to my contact information on the board and introduce myself as their teacher, musical director, and secretary, and as a fellow artist, composer, and improviser. I explain that they will all take on these same roles as the semester progresses.

JON: Before we introduce ourselves more personally, here is the Creative Workshop flyer, a welcome sheet about our workshop. Please read this now, and keep it in your folders. Note that we will be recording some of our work beginning in week 12.

Readers, your Creative Workshop flyer is in chapter 15, The Folder Chapter. Since you are now a virtual member of the workshop, please read the flyer on page 163.

COMMUNICATION 101
VERBAL INTRODUCTIONS

JON: Let's begin with some verbal introductions. Please introduce yourselves, and let us know of any talents and interests you may have. I will start things off. My name is Jon. I am from

Brooklyn, New York, where I was raised—or as I like to call it, "lowered." One of my favorite activities at the college is working with this workshop. I love my beautiful family, I love music, bird watching, and I was an art major in college.

The students—Roberto, Masty, Ezra, Yuto, Chester, Tim, and Bruno— introduce themselves, adding their hometowns and interests, and immediately our communication network is open! We find that in our workshop we have visual artists, a poet, a scientist, a student of magic, a dancer, and an avid cook.

JON: It's wonderful to hear that some of you are artists in various media as well as music. In the workshop we will draw upon those talents as well as various visual arts and performance art media. Also, let us know of any friends involved in the arts who may like to come and work with the workshop.

YUTO: I have a friend, Yumi, who is a sculptor. She studies at the Museum School. I will ask her if she would like to visit the workshop.

JON: That sounds great, Yuto.

Now that we are introduced, please keep this seating plan throughout the semester so that we know where everyone is for cueing. The only change is to create more of a curved shape so we can better see and hear each other.

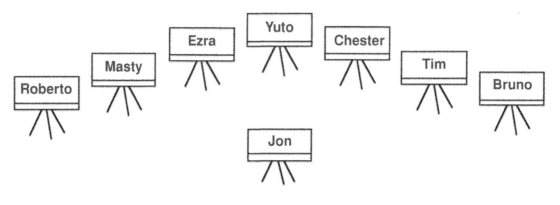

Fig. 1.1. CreW Seating Plan

Thank you CreW, that's perfect.

ARTISTIC INTRODUCTIONS

JON: Now that we know each other better at a verbal level, let's get to know each other on an artistic level. Roberto, may we begin with you? Since you are a musician, can you tell us more about yourself using your instrument? Your musical statement need not be long, not much longer than your verbal introduction.

Roberto hesitantly plays a slow, pretty series of chords, followed by Masty, who plays a fairly confident bluesy riff.

Then silence.

EZRA: I don't know what to do. Should I play part of a song?

I pose an interesting improvisatory challenge here to the workshop, asking them to use the medium of music to express something not motivated by music language—words such as "the Dorian mode" or a notated passage of music, or a chord symbol. It is the first time anyone has asked them to introduce themselves using music. I share a bit of workshop history.

JON: A number of years ago, a workshop student brought in a bouquet. She placed a flower in front of each of her colleagues and asked them each to play a solo statement inspired by his or her flower. Her workshop neighbor Paul looked at his flower and blurted out, "I don't know what to play. Put a C7 chord symbol in front of me and I'll show you something." And that he could. Paul was a very talented musician who could improvise through any chord progression, at any tempo, and in any odd meter. But this simple flower, a rose, stumped him. I asked him, "How would you describe this flower using words?" "It is pretty, soft, and fragrant," he responded. I directed him to translate his verbal description into music. He immediately, and sensitively, played some soft and pretty chords capped off with a light flurry of notes, and said, "That was fun." I simply had Paul translate his flower into language, a communication medium he understands, and from which he could play.

Ezra, how would you describe *you* with words?

EZRA: I am a quiet type, but can get nervous easily . . . and I love Brazilian music.

JON: Now translate your description into music.

Ezra begins playing shyly at first, and then builds to a fairly exciting rhythmic and harmonic cadence. His workshop colleagues respond with some verbal praise, and Ezra smiles at having opened up a nice communication channel for himself. The remaining introductions went smoothly.

> Readers, please introduce yourself to the rest of the workshop. Describe yourself with words, and then translate this description into your medium. Our spoken language is a powerful common medium between the arts. In fact, your personal written description may in itself be quite poetic, and inspire a painting, a dance, a drawing.

COMMUNICATION STUDIES

JON: Class, the following studies are communication studies that develop individual as well as group communication awareness. They will help our workshop gain confidence and enjoy our unique creative situation. Remember, this is our workshop. These sessions may, and should, be interrupted at any point to get feedback or suggestions.

> Imagine yourself as a "polyartist," an artist in all media. Dive into workshop ideas in as many media as you wish, not only your principal medium. Your body can

dance, sing, whistle, scat sing, grab a pencil and paper and sketch. If these are your first times trying, you'll be perfect at it. Here in the Creative Workshop we are all quite ingeniously perfect.

Mime Study

JON: CreW, we will begin our communication studies with Mime Study, a study that focuses awareness on the basic sound dimensions. Remember that everything we do in the workshop is a work in progress, and a healthy workshop is an interactive one, building ideas together.

CHESTER: What does "meem" mean?

JON: Mime is pronounced "meem" but is spelled M-I-M-E and is, in the words of the great French mime Marcel Marceau, "the art of silence." Mime is a theater art. Mime Study works with silence, beginning with playing an incredibly versatile instrument: the human body. By making our body an instrument, we actually touch and become the music. Our body can sing, dance, clap, shout, snap, whine, sniff, stomp, and lots more. Our body is an incredible pile of creations and inventions through which our creative ideas are realized. We simply have to get out of our own way. Our bodies are the instruments for this first take of the Mime Study. Later we can respond using our "regular" instruments or artistic medium. When I was a youngster, I developed an almost clairvoyant, ESP-like ability to speak the words someone was saying to me at exactly the same time they said them. Well, almost (it drove my Mom nuts!). Mime Study is something like that.

YUTO: Jon, you used the term "basic sound dimensions" a moment ago. What do you mean by that?

JON: The term "basic sound dimensions" refers to the essential spatial dimension-producing parameters of sound. "Dynamics," or the level of loudness of a sound, creates depth—how close or how far a sound is from the listener. "Rhythm," or the duration of a sound, creates the width, or time life, of a sound. "Direction" is a sound moving up or down in pitch, creating height—how high or low a sound is. "Articulation" (tone color), the manner of attack of a sound, creates the essential shape, roundness, or sharpness of a sound. These dimensions are always present but are often neglected by the music improviser as creative resources. In spoken language, these are the basic elements that create our speaking personality. Hearing the word "Hi" on the phone definitely means it's Mom calling, or an old or new friend. It's amazing how much character can be put into the delivery of a simple word, thanks to the basic sound dimensions.

And so, CreW, let's begin our Mime Study with one player who improvises using his or her body as a sound instrument. Singing, clapping, whining—any form of body sound expression is valid. The rest of the workshop, as exactly as possible, mimes the soloist silently. If the soloist is singing a powerful, bluesy lick, or quietly rubbing their palms together, the rest of the group mimes silently with only body motions. When the first soloist finishes, the next soloist begins to play his or her body, and the rest of the ensemble members, including the first soloist, mime silently with their bodies.

Let's try this. Roberto please be the first soloist, then Masty, and so forth.

Roberto begins creating some interesting body sounds. At this point, I often approach a workshop member who is listening intensely to the soloist but not moving silently to the soloist's sounds. I silently touch a student's hand to inspire some reaction. After one pass through the workshop, I mention, "Your ESP should be warming up nicely at this point." This comment stimulates some reactions.

TIM: I feel that I'm tapping into an ability that has been there all along.

JON: Good, Tim.

Two hands go up.

"I thought this would be simple!"

"Me too."

JON: Class, we spend so much time practicing at home, by ourselves, that interaction with another person or player takes some practice.

Now let's continue with another cycle. Let's gradually move from silent reflections of the soloist's sounds to actual sound reflections, until the entire ensemble is improvising together with body sounds. I will gradually cue each player back into silence to complete the first Mime Study.

The workshop begins and gradually connects as a group musically with the soloist.

ROBERTO: That is a lot of fun, but difficult at first.

JON: For soloists in Mime Study, dynamics, rhythm, direction, and articulation—the basic sound dimensions—naturally become a part of the music because we are in immediate contact with our bodies. As we clap our hands we really feel softness or loudness, and when singing a bluesy scat we feel it in our throats. As "silent" ensemble partners in Mime Study, we automatically reflect those sound dimensions with our bodies.

Now let's try Mime Study exactly as we just did, but using our instruments with our bodies. Yuto, can you start first? Remember, the rest of you be silent at first, but then begin to actually produce sounds with your instruments.

YUTO: May I play anything I want?

JON: Sure.

Yuto begins playing, and the workshop begins responding silently on their instruments to Yuto's sounds. Some of the group needs some silent coaching to get fingers and arms silently moving on their instruments. Gradually, CreW actually plays their instruments. Communication is happening. The piece ends with a rousing group improvisation.

Readers, Mime Study is a powerful performance theater piece, musically and visually. Try it in concert with your own group. Also try Mime Study as a performer or artist, communicating with your radio or stereo system. First, become the mime with your body, a dance reflecting the sounds. Then let your brush or your pencil become the mime reflecting the sounds on canvas or paper. The basic sound dimensions, the parameters of sound that create spatial dimension, may inspire you in your work. This may produce a nonrepresentational-looking work that is actually representational! Check out Harry Smith's *Manteca*, a painting he created in 1948 while listening to Dizzy Gillespie's classic tune "Manteca."

Try Mime Study with your own group situation in any art form. Dance is a very therapeutic activity, and helps our entire body become a creative vehicle. When doing Mime Study, you will find sounds that stimulate your creativity. Actors, find sound effects or music that suggests the scene of a script you are studying, and work with it.

JON: CreW, we are here to enjoy ourselves. The only wrong note or action you can produce in the workshop is a fearful one, or one that disregards the rest of the workshop. In the workshop, we are as strong as our weakest link. Speaking of links, let's try "Chains," another interesting communication study.

"Chains"

I like using "Chains" as a title for this study, a series of connected links. Linear motion and communication through the group is essential here. Linear motion refers to the chainlike beauty and life of language. In a sentence, a word tilts forward in momentum, dominoes to a next word, until a final cadence, or period. In the first variation of "Chains," each player is responsible for only one note, or link, of the musical chain. Let's try to make our chain, with each of us a single link, sound like the idea of one person. This study focuses on basic sound dimension awareness with our neighbors.

"Chains" Variation #1

1. Player one plays one note, or link.

2. Player two then plays a note, or the next link, at any point after player one, creating a dynamic, rhythmic, and directional connection to the first note of the chain.

3. Player three continues the chain.

Continue moving through the chain until a feeling of "oneness" begins to manifest itself. Player one, or a musical director, cues the last pass through the chain for an ending.

The workshop plays some of "Chains" Variation #1, and Chester waves his hand.

CHESTER: Would it be easier if we each had two or three notes to play as a link? More of a clear intention would be formed this way.

JON: You're right, Chester, we can try it with more notes, or "links," per player. The one note per link variation is more difficult but pulls us more into the moment. Let's try Chester's variation, using three notes per link. We can try the one-note link challenge again later.

"Chains" with Chester's Variation

In this second variation, each player is responsible for three notes per link of the music chain.

1. Player one plays three notes.

2. Player two plays the next three notes at any point after player one, creating a dynamic, rhythmic, directional, and articulation connection to the first link.

3. Player three continues the chain with three more notes.

Continue moving through the chain until player one, or the musical director, cues the last pass through the chain to its end for completion of the study.

Try any other variations you wish. Also, try adding a specific tonality or key as the group gains momentum with "Chains."

JON: Bravo, CreW. Chester is right, flow was easier to achieve since the three-note link motif gives more personality for the next player to work with.

> Readers, "Chains" can also work with two or more artists in any medium. Here is "Chains" for two or more poets sitting before a blank page.
>
> 1. Poet one writes a word, the first link.
>
> 2. Poet two writes the next word, the next link.
>
> Continue the cycle until the poem is completed by a link of silence.
>
> Adapt this activity to any medium you wish. For example: two artists, one canvas, and each brush stroke is a link of the chain.

JON: CreW, let's try another communication piece.

Sprecht-Blots

JON: "Sprecht-Blots" is my very-own-invented German word that means "Speak-Blots" in English. I thought it sounded cooler in German. You may have heard of Dr. Hermann Rorschach, the psychiatrist, and his inkblots, those black abstract images that he would flash at a patient and then say, "So tell me . . . what does this image make you think of?" Dr. Rorschach would study the patient's reactions to these inkblots and then make a diagnosis. "You are KA-

POOTZ, and need a good rest!" the good doctor might have said. This is the infamous Rorschach Test. In Sprecht-Blots, I will audibly flash, or speak, simple single words or phrases and have either a soloist or a group of players react musically. Let's try some Sprecht-Blots. These are some fun ones to start with. Play your immediate reaction.

> Join in here, my fellow painters, sketch artists, dancers, and actors. Get up, grab your bodies, brushes, and pencils, and react to these Sprecht-Blots. Take only about ten seconds of reaction to each Sprecht-Blot. Then move to the next Sprecht-Blot.

> Also, find a fellow painter, sketch artist, dancer, or actor, and sprecht some Sprecht-Blots at each other! Or find a group of painters. Have someone speak a Sprecht-Blot, and then bring together each painter's visual portrayal of the Sprecht-Blot, to produce an interesting group collage, a democratically inspired mural!

Air...... **Popcorn**...... *Snow*......... Desert...

PING PONG...... Ice Skating....... .... *BLIZZARD!*......

Mozzarella .... Rain....... Fog.......

MASTY: I loved doing that!

JON: Language is a wonderful medium to use as a creative catalyst. You guys did great on that, and you are blatantly text painting very well; what I mean is that your musical performance of the words (text painting) is using sounds that are obvious, or traditionally associated with these words and concepts. This is a good thing. Reacting in a totally opposite manner is cool also. Contrast. Close your eyes and imagine a video scene of Niagara Falls torrentially raging downward, crashing into the abyss below. Now, what would John Williams write as a soundtrack?

BRUNO: He would probably use a full French horn section, with tympani pounding away and the string section bowing their hearts out.

JON: Right, a blatant text (sound) painting of Niagara Falls. Now imagine the same scene, but with only a simple wooden flute playing an accompaniment as the soundtrack. An interesting contrast.

YUTO: I feel a strong sense of communication is being established today. I feel really free at times, and I wish I could feel that free when I am trying to play jazz, improvising over chord symbols.

JON: That's a great point. Remember that when playing any music, total awareness of the basic sound dimensions is important. For some of you, today may be the first time you considered the basic sound dimensions as an important part of your improvisation.

Several CreW members respond, "It is for me."

JON: Yuto, observe that when you are improvising over chord symbols, your attention may be distracted away from the basic sound dimensions.

YUTO: It certainly is. I am so busy trying to stay in the right place.

JON: With learning any new ability we have to practice until it becomes instinctive, as we do when learning a language, or learning how to ride a bicycle. In music learning and creating we can work intellectually, but we can still practice the ability to tap into the moment and work from the basic sound dimensions that our instinct has been responding to for years. That is part of what we've been doing today.

> I like to think of my intellect and instinct as very good friends; one teaches the other. The word "intellistinctual," another of my invented words, is how I like to think of it. I like "instinctuallectual," too. I don't agree with the "two sides of the brain" theories. I believe in "one mind" swirling with creative possibilities, the importance of observing and communicating these possibilities to ourselves and to others through our creative medium. This is an essential goal of this book.

STORY FORM

JON: Using a story or scenario to inspire music and art is nothing new and is known as programmatic music or program music. It is so not new that it can be traced back two and a half million years, which is why I thought story form an appropriate place to begin our creative explorations. Let's go back to the early cave peoples. Imagine an early cave-hunter returning excitedly from his first encounter with a woolly mammoth and trying to describe the hunt to his fellow clan members. The cave-hunter loudly sings "AAAAOOOORAHRRH!" mimicking the charging mighty mammoth. Then the descriptive hunter vocally expels "BOOOOMMMPH!!" with an excited jump as the beast falls into his well-placed pit-trap. Dinner is served!

BRUNO: The first scat singing!

JON: Right! Of course I would imagine that Luciano Pavarotti, the great opera singer, would not have been very impressed by this Paleolithic aria, but I bet the hunter's cave buddies were. This very same hunter may have done some of the beautiful cave paintings inspired by such stories.

"THE CORONATION"

JON: As a foundation for our music and art we can use stories. Old stories, new, sad, blue, or happy stories, poetry, and prose work equally well. To wrap up our first week of the workshop, let's try some story form to stimulate our music and art inspirations. For this first story we will again step back in time to, let's say, the seventeenth century, a cathedral, and a coronation. You must pardon me, I always get choked up at coronations.

MASTY: Who is getting crowned?

JON: Well, actually, a king *and* a queen are being crowned. How would you like to be Queen Mastaneh, Masty?

Masty likes that idea.

JON: Any volunteers for the king?

Ezra's hand shoots up.

JON: Great, King Ezra, I like it. CreW, you will be using the basic sound dimensions and your communication skills, which should be warmed up from earlier challenges in today's session.

TIM: Jon, where did you get this story?

JON: This mini-opera is from my imagination.

"The Coronation: Act One"

JON: This piece calls for a queen, Mastaneh, a king, Ezra, four villagers, and a cathedral scene player.

ROBERTO: I love cathedrals!

JON: Okay, Roberto, you will portray the cathedral scene. Bruno, Yuto, Tim, and Chester will be the villagers. Roberto, we need for you to set up some cathedral ambience.

ROBERTO: How about some blatant text painting here—some bells and some nice creaky sounds?

JON: Sounds perfect. Villagers, you are a choir. We will begin with a simple, slow chorale in E minor tonality, played in simple quarter notes. Imagine you are processioning up the aisle of this great seventeenth-century cathedral. Softly, slowly, and in quarter notes only, ready, *one . . . two . . . three . . . four.*

The chorale of villagers is playing nicely. I gently stop them for a moment.

JON: That sounds great, villagers. For the rest of the chorale, let's intensify the rhythmic and textural interest. Villagers, you will begin in quarter notes as we just rehearsed. On my cue, Bruno and Yuto, begin to add eighth-note rhythms along with the quarter notes and play in contrary motion to each other.

YUTO: What do you mean by contrary motion?

JON: If Bruno is playing his line in an ascending, upward manner, you play in a descending, downward manner, and vice versa. Yuto and Bruno, try that briefly, *one . . . two . . . three . . . four.*

Nice job, guys! Tim and Chester, at that same cue you begin to use eighth notes along with quarter notes and play a direction canon. That simply means you echo each other's direction.

TIM: Something like "Frère Jacques"?

JON: Right, but don't worry about getting the same pitches. Just try for direction similarity.

Now let's discuss the roles of our soon-to-be royalty. King Ezra, at some point during the opening quartet chorale I want you to enter and play a solo—an aria, actually—in E major, and in lower register. Think of a bass or baritone human voice. Play in a spoken, rhythmic manner. Play proudly—you are the king! At the king's entrance, villagers switch the chorale to E major and play softly under King Ezra. After a bit, Queen Mastaneh enters and improvises an aria in a higher, mezzo-soprano register. Gradually the king and queen join together in a musical conversation. Continue this dialogue, this exchange, and build in intensity until you reach a climax portrayed with a sustained, long, loud trilled note. Villagers, join your new king and queen and also play a long, loud trilled note, all together. Watch me for a direct cut-off. This will be a dramatic conclusion of act one of "The Coronation."

Okay, CreW, let's try "The Coronation: Act One," from the top.

After a nice rendition of act one, I congratulate the workshop.

JON: Brava e bravo, Queen Mastaneh and King Ezra! That was well done.

BRUNO: Wow! As a villager I really had to listen deeply to stay in contrary motion communication with Yuto.

JON: Awareness of direction, in this case contrary motion direction, is a desired motion between melodic lines in composition and counterpoint studies, and creates a sense of independence and depth.

Ensemble directors, try "The Coronation: Act One" with various instrument combinations. I once did this with one king and two queens. It got ugly. In chapter 14, the CreW On the Road chapter, I will share with you a wonderful "Coronation" experience in Italy.

Dance ensemble directors, I would love to see the simple scenario of "The Coronation: Act One" as the choreography for a dance troupe. The simple language used translates easily into visual relationships: contrary motion in an even, rhythmic manner, build in intensity, and canon (which is actually a term used in choreography to indicate a particular movement done by different dancers at different times). I tried "The Coronation" myself as a solo dancer. I had fun, and I can't even dance!

ASSIGNMENTS FOR WEEK 2

JON: During the week, find a story or a poem—steal one if needed, or make one up. That is your choice. Use it as a foundation for a piece for next week. How you translate your story into any medium is up to you. In "The Coronation" various techniques are used: blatant text painting to describe the cathedral ambience; traditional music language; choosing the key of E minor to guide the villagers tonally; and simple verbal language—words like up and down—to guide their interplay, and gender to guide register choices for the king and queen.

Please provide a hard copy of your ideas for your colleagues to follow and make enough copies to go around.

ANOTHER COMMUNICATION STUDY

JON: Here is another communication study that I would like all of you to try during the week to work on your personal communication development. In all your verbal conversations with others, show a true interest in what they are saying. Let them teach you something. When others sense this, they will let you teach them something. A healthy dialogue will result. You will find that the best true improvisers make the best conversationalists.

I also want you to observe your interaction with others in rehearsals, ensemble classes, and performances. Are you observing and reacting to your fellow performers as well as you observe yourself? Your reaching out will inspire them, in turn, to respond to you.

> My fellow polyartists, are you aware of all media, all around you, in the environment, in the work of your fellow artists? Always keep this dialogue open. A great way to stretch your imagination is to do things you would never do: read a book you wouldn't usually read, or go to a movie you would never see. It might inspire a satire. These are great environments for fresh ideas. Strike up a conversation with someone you would never talk to. You just may fall in love.

JON: Have a great week, and one important thing. If you are not able to come to class, please send someone to substitute for you. Your fellow workshop members may need a full workshop to support their ideas. It is nice to give someone else a CreW experience.

Thanks CreW.

> Readers, I feel good about this group, a nice mix of personalities and healthy curiosities, a great cast of characters, a nice recipe for a successful workshop.

CHAPTER 2 – WEEK 2
COMMUNICATION *201* AND STORY FORM

We don't see [hear] things as they are, we see [hear] them as we are.

—Anais Nin

WEEK 1 REVIEW

JON: I hope you had a good week, my fellow workshop members, and enjoyed last week's activities.

Here is a cute CreW-on-the-road story. I was recently invited to visit Foxborough High School to perform in concert and to conduct a Creative Workshop session. In the session I tried "The Coronation," the story form piece we played last week, and as I assigned parts I asked a girl at the piano, "Would you like to be the queen?"

"Sure," she brightly accepted.

"And what is your name?" I asked of the soon-to-be-royalty.

"Victoria," she replied.

I gasped. "Queen Victoria! Who just happens to be the longest reigning monarch in British history!"

Thanks for letting me share that.

CreW, I hope your verbal and musical conversations with others took on an enhanced level of communication during the week.

BRUNO: Jon, it's amazing how little I listen to what others are saying.

EZRA: And playing.

JON: Thank you for your observations. Daily activities such as breathing, eating, drinking, and taking a walk are also great opportunities for working on individual communication skills. You'll feel, taste, enjoy, and learn a lot more. On your walks through the city, open up your field of view and check out the incredible architectural details Boston has to offer. Someone had to get up real high to create that stuff. And what are all those mysterious, one-inch-ish wide, circular black and sometimes gray spots all over the city's sidewalks? Be observant. Be curious. Curiosity is part of creative consciousness. As I mentioned in last week's introduction, I love to watch birds. I love the "hunt" involved in finding birds by sight and sound. To be good at this sport and all sports, one must be totally in the moment.

Before we take a look at and listen to our new story form ideas, let's warm up with some more communication goodies.

COMMUNICATION 201
"WHAT GOES UP . . ." STUDY

JON: CreW, what do archery, sneezes, and bowling all have in common?

TIM: They all have seven letters.

JON: That's true, Tim, but . . .

BRUNO: They all build up intensity and then let go?

JON: Yes. Can you put it more simply?

BRUNO: Uh, tension and release?

JON: That's better. And simpler yet?

BRUNO: Cadence?

JON: Right. Here is a simple quotation.

> *Music is motion from nonrest to rest.* —Olivier Messiaen

Olivier Messiaen's quote will be our theme for this communication study I call "What Goes Up . . ." Study.

Cadence—movement from nonrest to rest—can be subjective, and that's the fun part of this study. Tim and Masty, on my downbeat, I would like you both to simply begin playing together. Observe your interchange. When you hear a cadence, a movement to rest, simply stop playing. OK? Ready, play.

Tim and Masty play for a while, wide-eyed and concentrating, and then happen to move in contrary motion to an octave, where they both briefly smile, and stop.

JON: Very good for your first try. Good focus. Now, Ezra and Yuto, please try this. Begin playing on the downbeat.

They begin playing rather quickly and intensely together, and after a bit Ezra simplifies his rhythm, Yuto follows suit, Ezra plays a repeated note, Yuto moves by step, and they successfully come to rest.

JON: Wow. You guys are really listening. Let's raise the ante and try this concept with a quartet. Roberto, Chester, Masty, and Tim, on the downbeat, ready, play.

Within several seconds three members of the quartet find a fairly obvious cadence, but one player continues playing, creating intensity again. This happens several times. I interrupt.

JON: Hold it, quartet!

MASTY: We had a cadence a few times, I thought, and then we lost it.

CHESTER: It's really hard for me to concentrate on everyone.

JON: Right, Chester, and that's the challenge in these communication pieces. The more we can be listening to our neighbors, the more efficient we become since we can draw on their creative ideas. When everyone is doing this it can be magical. Remember, it takes two to tango, and one to un-tango. Everyone must be listening intently, feeling his or her playing relationship to the whole. It only takes one player to knock over the resting point, so to speak. This is a difficult study, but you guys are doing great. Let's try the same quartet, once more. Concentrate. Ready? Play.

The quartet plays several quick, powerful, dissonant attacks, almost together rhythmically, and then softens, slows, and arrives at a fairly beautiful resting point several attacks later, and stops.

JON: Bravo, CreW! That was impressive.

ROBERTO: I love the sounds we are producing, and they are all new ideas.

JON: That's right, Roberto. And we have lots more to find!

> Speaking of "it takes two to tango, and one to un-tango": Dancers and nondancers, grab a dance partner and try the "What Goes Up . . ." Study. Each of you silently imagine yourselves doing a dance, any kind of dance. On cue, at the same time, each of you begin that imagined dance. Observe your dancing and that of your partner, and continue your dancing until you both reach a mutual "cadence" or point of meeting or rest. Again, cadence can be very subjective. Trying this with a larger dance group would really be cool. I always think of the dynamic of a funnel when working with the "What Goes Up . . ." Study—ideas pour into the funnel, at first disparate, but gradually move to a central focus.

STORY FORMS
HAIKU: JAPANESE POETRY—FURUIKE YA (OLD POND)

JON: Let's dive into the story form ideas you have created. Who would like to begin?

YUTO: Jon, I have an idea to share.

JON: Go right ahead.

YUTO: You mentioned that the story could be in the form of a poem, so I brought in a haiku for us to work with. Here are some copies of a haiku, a type of Japanese poetry. This haiku named "Old Pond" was written by Bashō, a famous haiku master. I have translated the lines of the haiku into English for you below the Japanese, and I would like the class to create some music from it. Each player is to be a part of the scene, as I will indicate. I will not need the entire workshop for this piece. I want it to be as simple as possible.

JON: That's a good point, Yuto; remember that your works need not include the entire workshop. Solos and duets work great, depending on your creative needs.

YUTO: Chester, can you be the frog? Ezra, you can be the water sound, and Tim, you can be the pond itself. I would like to recite the haiku in Japanese, and have the class play along. Is everyone clear about your parts?

EZRA: Is blatant text painting okay?

JON: It sure is; you can interpret your role any way you wish. Just focus on our ongoing theme of communication within yourself and through the workshop. Let's try it.

YUTO: Roberto, you are the atmosphere in the haiku. Can you create an introduction, and when I begin reading, everyone please react.

Furuike Ya (Old Pond)
by Matsuo Bashō
furuike ya
kawazu tobi komu
mizu no oto

(English translation)

Old Pond
A frog jumps
The sound of water

On cue Roberto creates a beautiful, atmospheric setting. Yuto recites the text in Japanese, and Ezra, Tim, and Chester begin to play their roles. After a moment I interrupt the workshop.

JON: Remember that dynamics may be the most powerful basic sound dimension. If we are too loud, all the other dimensions are obscured. Make sure Yuto's voice is clearly heard. It's easy to get involved in your own playing. Remember, you are each a part of the haiku. Again, please.

Roberto begins again, Yuto recites, and everyone portrays the three simple lines of the haiku beautifully.

TIM: I liked that, but can we try it again? I didn't feel as connected as I would like to be in my role as the pond.

The workshop explores some more variations of the haiku, and the story forms are off to a great start.

> Visual artists, how would you translate the classic haiku "Old Pond" with your brush, pencil, or clay? Take the same amount of time it takes to speak the haiku. Dancers, try portraying "Old Pond" with your bodies; actors, with your faces. Try a number of variations of "Old Pond" in your medium.

YUTO: Thank you, workshop, for playing the haiku. My friend Yumi, the sculptor I mentioned last week, would love to visit and work with us.

JON: That sounds great, Yuto, and thanks to Yumi also. We will have a guest week, and I'll give Yumi a special, reserved spot. Does anyone have another idea for a story form?

"THE VILLAGE"

BRUNO: Jon, I have a story form that actually happened to me.

JON: Let's hear it.

BRUNO: My father is a photojournalist, and as a child I traveled with him. From these travels I have an exciting memory that I think will make a nice piece. I don't have a hard copy.

JON: That's fine, Bruno. For now, we will listen to your story. As workshop ideas for portraying your story come up, please sketch them down to create a hard copy.

First, tell us your story.

BRUNO: On a trip to Africa with my father, we spent a couple of days in a small village which consisted of several homes that created a circle around a central circular fireplace that was the hub of the village. In the evenings, after dinner, a fire would be built and many of the families would sing and dance together. One evening, after the group music ended and the families returned to their homes, my dad and I stayed at the fireplace to talk, and an incredible sound event occurred. For about an hour, while the families were slowly winding down in their homes from the group activities, we could hear all around us wonderful sounds—some singing, some instrument playing, along with excited conversation. From our central vantage point, we could hear a rich tapestry of sound that the villagers produced. Can we try to capture that sound with our workshop?

JON: Sure. Do you have any starting ideas?

BRUNO: Yes, I do. Each of us will represent a family in their home. But how do we create that rich mix of sounds?

JON: The effect you heard that evening was rich and powerful because each home had its own life of sound and momentum. A song drifted from one home, another home had an instrument playing another piece of music, an argument coming from another home, a baby crying at the next, and so forth. So let us use your excellent starting idea. Each of us will portray a family. First, I would like each of you to conceive, silently, of the sound activities in your home. Make it in the form of a simple statement, a repeated or looped musical groove of some kind, using your instruments.

MASTY: Can we also sing and dance?

JON: Great idea. In fact, imagine a dance to do with the rest of your body as you play your groove. On my cue, I want you to begin to dance and play the ideas together.

CHESTER: That would sound terrible! Things wouldn't be together, and I can't dance!

JON: First of all, Chester, we would never play terrible music in our workshop, and the musical magic that Bruno heard that night was due to the rich layers of individual sounds from the various family activities. Keep the dance simple if you wish. I want folks to sing and dance in the workshop. When we sing and dance, our bodies become instruments, touching and becoming the music. Let's hear if this works. Does everyone have an idea? Go ahead and silently finger your instruments to solidify your idea, and imagine your dance. On my downbeat, everyone simply start playing your idea and try your dance at the same time. This is one piece in which I *do not* want you to communicate with your neighbors. Stick to *your* idea. Do *not* be moved by your neighbor's tempo or tonality or dance. The *only* dimension I want you to work with is dynamics. Create a balance with your neighbors so that the rich layers can be heard.

Let's stand and spread out and create a circle for this. Ready? Play.

I cue the workshop to begin. The students excitedly play their ideas and dance. From my vantage point at the "hub" of the room, the effect sounds and looks great. After a minute or so, I stop the group.

JON: We are off to a great start.

CHESTER: It was easier for me to focus on my groove than I thought, and dancing was fun.

JON: Are you happy with the effect, Bruno? You're the composer.

BRUNO: Yes, I like it. Could you have each of us play louder at times so that we can hear each family's groove? I would also like for us to sing at some point. I hope this is not too much to ask.

JON: Not at all. CreW, this is a good opportunity to introduce some workshop hand signals to you. Here is a hand signals dictionary. We will be using these hand signals throughout the semester.

Readers, please take a look at your hand signals dictionary handout on page 165 of chapter 15, The Folder Chapter. Having your group on the same page with clear visual cues is important and gives the director more control.

JON: Take a moment right now and refer to the start and stop, dynamics, singing indications, and tonal cues in the hand signals dictionary. These signals will come in handy right now.

BRUNO: As you were studying the hand signals dictionary, I quickly sketched a scenario for "The Village" based on our ideas. I will put this in a clearer form and have hard copies for next week to put in our folders.

The Village
Each of you is a family in their simple homes in a village
full of family sounds and energy.

Silently conceive of a repetitive groove figure and a dance, in any tempo
and in any tonality that you wish, using your instrument/voice/body.

On cue, everyone begin your groove and dance, and maintain
your groove no matter what is happening around you.

We want a rich effect here.
Balance dynamically with the other players.

Jon will cue various players to play louder or
softer so we can enjoy taking a peek into
each player's home groove.

Jon will also cue for the group to sing a long
tone (sing until you are out of breath)
or to sing active percussive sounds.

Continue to play your groove and dance as you sing.

For the last section, Jon will give extraction cues.
In this case, on a cue, extract just a little of your groove
and your dance each time
until gradually you are left with nothing.
When there is silence and no motion,
Jon will give a cue for a final long tone sung by everyone that will
naturally bring the piece to a close.
FINE

JON: Okay, CreW, let's try it. Those grooves you played when we tried "The Village" the first time worked nicely. Ready, everyone? I will give a cue for us to begin together.

The workshop plays, dances, and sings with gusto, and the ideas work well. Focusing dynamically on each player's groove is powerful, and the long tone singing is dramatic, especially the final long sung tone that naturally moves to silence.

JON: Great job, everyone.

CHESTER: That was intense. The dancing and the singing with the groove helped my sense of time. I really liked that.

A BRIEF LOOK AT OPEN THEATER

ROBERTO: In these story form pieces I feel like an actor as much as a musician.

JON: Good observation, Roberto. Throughout the semester, we will draw inspiration from various art media, from visual art and dance art and, with story form, acting. In the dramatic arts there is an analogous workshop to our Creative Workshop called Open Theater. In Open Theater workshops, actors are challenged to become weapons and colors, and in one technique, the actors become an actual orchestra reacting with their voices and bodies to the bodily movements of a "conductor." Similarly to our techniques, Open Theater brings a heightened awareness of a situation to the actor. Robert Pasolli's *A Book on the Open Theatre* is filled with wonderful ideas that can inspire our music.

And now, CreW, in our next story form our musical acting roles will be as preachers and congregation members of a small country church.

"REVEREND KELLY'S BAPTIST CHURCH"

JON: Let's close up today's story form session with "Reverend Kelly's Baptist Church." The setting is a small, simple Baptist church. The character roles are simple: a preacher and the congregation of the church. I can't remember the movie scene that inspired this piece, but it was the interplay of preacher and congregation that I found captivating: the preacher preaching away, almost singing the sermon, the response from the faithful, then the preacher, then the faithful, preacher, faithful, building to a wonderful, intense, swirling sense of activity. Reverend Tim, would you like to be the preacher?

TIM: Me?

JON: Yes. Simply imagine yourself talking with your guitar.

TIM: Can I use bluesy licks?

JON: Sure, that makes sense since blues, a lyric form, is traditionally inspired by storytelling.

"Reverend Kelly's Baptist Church" begins with "We Shall Overcome," inspired by a gospel song by the Reverend Charles Tindley and popularized by Pete Seeger and Zilphia Horton, among others. In the 1960s, the song became an anthem of the Civil Rights Movement.

REVEREND KELLY'S BAPTIST CHURCH

We Shall Overcome

traditional from a gospel tune by Charles Tindley

Fig. 2.1. "We Shall Overcome"

Hum "We Shall Overcome" two times for an introduction.

After completion of "We Shall Overcome," the appointed preacher begins to preach with their instrument.

Preacher, create clear phrases for the congregation to react to.

Congregation, play and vocalize simple responses to the preacher.

Continue and quicken this dialogue, slowly building in intensity.

Build until preacher and congregation are playing together.

When it feels like a climax, look for a cutoff.

After the cutoff, return to "We Shall Overcome" for an ending.

For the last bar, hold on the IV chord.

Play some fills, then cut off, and then play a final chord and closing fills.
FINE

JON: Let's rehearse this. Give us a simple C major triad for pitch, Masty. Let's do the hymn twice for now, nice and slow, *one, two, three, four . . .*

The workshop hums fairly well here.

JON: Nice job. The form is simple: first, the introduction with our "choir," then the dialogue between Reverend Tim and the congregation. Please use your instruments along with your voices for your responses to Reverend Tim. Let's try it. *Three, four, and . . .*

The introduction goes nicely, and Tim starts preaching with some nice voicelike bluesy licks on his guitar with no pauses, and continues and continues. I gently interrupt.

JON: Excuse me, Reverend Tim. Can you put a period in once in a while?

TIM: What do you mean by a period?

JON: As in language, come to the end of a musical sentence; let your phrase take a breath so the congregation can be inspired by your sermon and respond. Let's try it again.
Three, four . . .

Tim really creates some nice bluesy phrases with clear pauses and the congregation responds.

JON: Sorry to stop you again. Nice job, Tim. Congregation, don't play too long in your responses to Tim, or too loudly at first. We need room to build the dialogue rhythmically and dynamically. Try just "one word" musical responses at first. Like *yeah!* or *Amen!* with your instruments. Let it build from there. Ready? When the dialogue reaches a high point I will give a cut. Then let's all hum that intro as an ending, adding our instrument to our voices also. Ready, let's try this.

CreW plays nicely here, patiently building the dialogue and reaching a fairly intense frenzy. I cut the ensemble, give a conducted *three, four,* and the choir hums and plays "We Shall Overcome" two times. Just before the final bar I shout "F7!" and give a cue and hold the workshop there. Folks play some bluesy stuff. I give a cut and cue the final chord, and the workshop plays a rousing mixture of final fills.

JON: Nice job. I feel that the whole piece was played excellently.

EZRA: Jon, may I be the reverend for the recording?

JON: On pieces with specified soloists perhaps we can choose soloists aleatorically.

CreW looks puzzled.

JON: The term "aleatoric" refers to decision-making done using a chance operation such as a coin toss. We will have a week in which I will introduce one of my own aleatoric pieces.

MASTY: Like John Cage's work.

JON: Yes, he is noted for his use of aleatoric means in his pieces.

BRUNO: Jon, I noticed that you used traditional notation in "Reverend Kelly's Baptist Church." I didn't realize we could use regular notation. There were times in "The Village" that I wanted to use notation. It's more exacting than just using words.

JON: I actually wanted us to try to use words as our "notation" technique so that we could explore their potential. You are right, traditional notation does create a clear guide for a musical idea for the performer. It gives the composer more control. But as you have noticed, using "word" notation, as in our story form pieces, also works well to build a piece of music. This technique puts more compositional control in the hands of the performers. I'm happy you brought that up, Bruno, because with our next theme, Expanding Traditional Notation, we will be using our good old traditional notation language.

> Actors and dancers, "Reverend Kelly's Baptist Church" would translate well as a dance piece, or as a dramatic improvisational dialogue. The call-and-response rhythm of the scene can be interpreted in many ways. This is what the great Dixieland ensembles were all about: congregational communication.

> I bet Jackson Pollock would paint the heck out of this scene. I can imagine him tossing the color red for the preacher's statements (calls) and tossing other colors for the congregation's responses, and building in intensity. Nice rhythm and contrast.

JON: CreW, before I discuss our next theme, I would like to start a collaborative composition that we will continue through the semester. It's called "Democratic Chorale." Please take out some manuscript paper.

"DEMOCRATIC CHORALE"

JON: For this piece we need to use traditional notation for building the foundation. This is a democratically prepared piece, so majority rules, and we will be voting right now.

I would like each of you to choose—silently—any note to play, and on my cue we will all play these notes together, creating a chord. Upon hearing this chord, raise your hand if you *like* this chord.

TIM: Are we looking for a pretty chord?

JON: I will leave that up to the voters. Let's play our first notes together and see if we can reach a majority of four or more positive votes. Let's play the first chord. On the downbeat and . . . now.

An interesting chord results and one hand pops up.

JON: No majority, so let's try again. Choose another note and play.

Another interesting chord and five hands pop right up and a sixth slowly joins in.

JON: A majority; write that note down on your manuscript paper. Now, let's try for a second chord for our chorale. On my cue, please play the first note you just wrote down, our first majority decision, and follow it with a new second note of your choice. Then vote on the second chord.

CreW needs several tries before agreeing on the second chord of our Democratic Chorale.

JON: Let's try for a third chord, and then we can put this in our folders. We will add on to our chorale in future workshop meetings.

BRUNO: How long should the chorale be?

JON: We will also put that to a vote later.

> In the art of music, generally a group of musicians, from two to one hundred, work together. This is a perfect setting for what I call "democreative activities." "Democratic Chorale" is one possibility; a musical action is taken and the group takes a vote. In other media, such as theater and dance, group art exists, and more democreative possibilities also exist. The fantastic collaborative theater works of artist Robert Rauschenberg, choreographer Merce Cunningham, and composer John Cage come to mind. In the visual art world artists generally work by themselves, though there are notable exceptions. Claude Monet and Frédéric Bazille's powerful relationship helped to create the style of Impressionism. Jean-Michel Basquiat and Andy Warhol's collaboration was notable as well. In some Asian art traditions a painter would begin a work and pass it on to another artist to continue the work. In fact we tried some poetic and music collaborations with "Chains" during our first meeting.

JON: Right now, I'd like to talk about one of my favorite hobbies, reading music.

CHESTER: Reading music!? How can reading music be a hobby? Hobbies are supposed to be fun. I find reading music a lot of work!

JON: Yes, Chester—when first learning any new language, there is some tedium, and a commitment is needed. But after time, and with study, a language becomes purely instinctive. With your commitment, reading music will become as instinctive as spoken language. Here is a brief pep talk about traditional notation.

TRADITIONAL NOTATION

JON: The traditional music notation language, employing a staff—a group of lines upon which to indicate pitches and rhythms—is an ingenious one. This notation language does a wonderful job of portraying a composer's intentions. I strongly encourage everyone to attain a high level of literacy in traditional notation, not only as composers but also as performers and improvisers. Most musical works were at first conceived, then improvised and worked out with some instrument, and finally sketched down. In the past, before recording technology, notation was the only way composers could document ideas or communicate them to people not immediately present. Check out this scenario: Imagine handing a musician who is not familiar with the music of Bill Evans a transcription of one of his improvised solos, let's say Bill's classic solo on "Come Rain or Come Shine." Have them study the notation and learn it. Then tell them it was an improvisation. They would probably be pretty surprised. Music reading ability is also a powerful improvisational art.

MASTY: How can you call reading music improvisation, when the written music is telling you what to play?

JON: There is a lot that the notation doesn't tell the reader. A master sight-reader is so in the moment that she can, at first sight, interpret and play the written notes, making them work musically, blending rhythmically, dynamically, and with proper articulation, all at the same time. To hear and feel one's part in the whole musical picture, reacting efficiently and musically to what is happening around you, is a truly strong improvisatory ability. Working from a cold, lifeless piece of paper! Magical.

Music literacy is a wonderful resource for improvisation. Read the melody of a tune, and also use some of that melodic material in your improvisation. Visualize and play a counterpoint under that melody. Accompany the melody with chords and lead notes that support the melody. Grab some rhythmic ideas from the tune. The possibilities are endless. As you can see, I'm a big fan of music literacy. Having this ability has truly been one of the most important music resources for me professionally, helping my performance, teaching, and compositional careers.

For CreW, traditional notation will be just one of a number of our "notation" techniques. Since we're on the subject, here is a Sight-Reading Bibliography for you to put in your folders. I hope you put those books to good use.

> Fellow music artists, you may want to take a look at the Sight-Reading Bibliography that is in your workshop folder in chapter 15 on page 168. The bibliography addresses gaining reading abilities from three perspectives: as performers, as observers, and as if you were an instrument.
>
> One of my favorite improvisatory studies is to approach playing a line of melody as an actor would practice delivering a line from Shakespeare—working that line repeatedly, breathing life into it, shaping that line with the basic sound dimensions. I enjoy telling people that I feel that some of the greatest improvisers are the classical music masters. The ability to breathe powerful life into an inanimate sheet of paper is an incredible art, separating the master from the student. Some Glenn Gould, anyone?

EXPANDING TRADITIONAL NOTATION AND WRITTEN LANGUAGE

JON: For our next topic for our creative music explorations we will look at traditional notation as a creative medium that can be stretched, cut, rotated, hybridized, and poked, not unlike a lump of clay. For our first work with traditional notation we will create freshly notated ideas or borrow notated ideas, and use them in a fresh manner.

YUTO: What do you mean by "fresh" Jon, like bread?

JON: By "fresh" I mean new. I will show you ideas from your CreW ancestors that use traditional notation as their basic medium but *expand* the notation possibilities. Some of these ideas may seem strange to you at first. This is a good thing. Strange is new. New is good. New is fresh. Fresh is healthy. Good, fresh, healthy music.

Does anyone have a fake book or tune book that I may borrow for a moment? Thanks, Roberto.

I hold up the book for the class.

JON: Think of this pile of pages, the notes and chords on them, as your lump of clay to work with; lots of ideas here to use in lots of possible ways.

QUODLIBET: ARTISTIC PICKPOCKETING

JON: The ideas I will show today are just scratching the surface of notation-expanding possibilities. I present them simply as catalyst for your imaginations. Let's begin with a simple, efficient use of notation. We can call this technique "blending" or "cross-breeding." Actually, there is an official musical term, "quodlibet," that can be used here, which simply means to quote freely another person's musical idea—basically steal!

"Yesterday/Yesterdays"

JON: Brad, a CreW member from several semesters ago, came in with this idea. He told the class, "I went looking through my fake book and opened to these two facing pages. The Lennon & McCartney tune 'Yesterday' was sitting on the left and 'Yesterdays,' the Jerome Kern tune, was on the right. One tune is in F major, the other in D minor, a nice relative relationship. I thought we could just play them both at the same time and hear what happens." "That's it?," I responded to Brad. At first I thought, What a lazy oaf. What an easy way to do this assignment. But then I thought, maybe he has something here. Let's play Brad's idea right now and hear what happens. Yuto and Masty, here is a lead sheet for "Yesterday" for you to share. Roberto and Tim, here is a sheet for "Yesterdays." Chester and Bruno, a "Yesterday" for you, and Ezra, a "Yesterdays" for you. Some of you take the melody line, some of you the chords.

CHESTER: Isn't this going to sound pretty weird?

JON: Remember, Chester, we don't play "weird" music in CreW. We call it "inventive" music. Music with a stroke of genius may be a more optimistic description. Let's try Brad's idea. Chord players, keep your chords simple. This will help the "harmonic hybridizations" taking place. Let's try it nice and slow, and pretty. For now we will play until the longer form "Yesterday" has completed one chorus. "Yesterdays" players, repeat to the top of your form as needed. Ready . . . *three, four* . . .

As they play the two tunes simultaneously, there are various vocal reactions moving through the workshop. Upon completion, reactions are mixed.

"Parts of that were pretty wild."

"It was quite beautiful for some strange reason."

JON: Class, each tune is well composed. Each layer has a powerful momentum, which helps the hybridization work. Remember, the registrar of the college calls our Creative Workshop Ensemble an Advanced Performance Lab, and rightfully so—a lab, a laboratory—and we certainly are experimenting, my fellow musical explorers. The technique we are using here with "Yesterday/Yesterdays" is not new. Composers will bring seemingly disparate bits of music together in different keys, called polytonality, and in different tempos, called polymetric. Since here we are using two different tunes, we can call this poly*tune*ality. Two of the masters of the art of quodlibet are the great jazz saxophonist Dexter Gordon and the composer Charles Ives.

"KNOM" Variations

JON: Here is one more notation "experiment" I would like to share with you. To develop this composition "KNOM," I printed a jazz lead sheet on a clear plastic sheet in order to get various views of the original music—the original view, the original upside-down view, the original turned over view, and the original turned over and upside-down views—so many variations we may need Dramamine to read them! Thelonious Monk's "Epistrophy" is being used as the foundation to create this new melodic line.

After playing through the clear plastic sheet possibilities, the workshop finally decides on the original turned-over version, and our humble egos actually like it better than the original melody. Sorry, Thelonious. Here are the first four bars of "KNOM." CreW enjoys playing this line and the original line as a duet. That clear plastic sheet really expanded our "vision" and composition possibilities.

Fig. 2.2. "KNOM"

Poetical Variations

Let's try the techniques used here with our own traditional spoken and written language. The Creative Workshop did a study titled "Yesterday/Yesterdays" using quodlibet technique playing two classic standard compositions, similar in title and tonal center, together—in a sense, cross-breeding the two songs.

Let's try quodlibet with some poetry as working materials. Find two poems similar in theme and hold them next to each other. When you glance back and forth between them, do any interesting text connections occur? Create a fresh poem from them.

Here's a little poem I bred from American and English poetry stock, Joyce Kilmer's "Trees" and A. E. Housman's "Loveliest of Trees." I apologize to poets out there, but I actually had fun writing this.

To See a Tree

To see a tree that
May not come again
A tree hung with bloom
Upon her leafy arms
Who stands against the earth
And by fools like me

Thanks to Monique-Adelle for giving me Lang Eliot's book *Music of the Birds,* which is filled with bird-inspired poetry. Here's another poetical hybridization using Percy Bysshe Shelley's "To a Skylark" and Edith Thomas's evensong poem, "The Vesper Sparrow." Of course, connection is another very subjective word.

Higher still and higher
Against the fading west.
Like a cloud of fire
Dives and finds a nest.

ASSIGNMENT FOR WEEK 3

JON: So, CreW, there are many different possibilities for expanding traditional notation and our written and spoken language. We scratched a beginning today. For next week, find your own special way to use and expand on these incredible languages. Remember that wonderful ideas will appear when you least expect it. Keep your ears and eyes open.

CHAPTER 3 — WEEK 3
EXPANDING THE TRADITIONAL NOTATION LANGUAGE

Language exerts hidden power, like a moon on the tides.

—Rita Mae Brown

JON: Good morning, CreW. I am still excited about last week's story form pieces. Thank you for your ideas and for playing the pieces so well.

EZRA: Jon?

JON: Yes?

EZRA: I have a band, and before a rehearsal, I tried Mime Study with them. At first they were hesitant, but gradually they relaxed and enjoyed the experience, and the rehearsal went pretty well also. Your pep talk inspired me to find a buddy to practice reading traditional music notation with.

JON: Good, Ezra. Duo playing is great for working on improvisation also.

EZRA: And, I believe I know what those black and gray, as well as pink, spots are all over the city sidewalks . . . chewing gum?

JON: I think you may be right. Who ever would have thought that many people chewed gum, and were litterbugs!

EXPANDING THE TRADITIONAL NOTATION LANGUAGE

JON: How did everyone do with your expanding traditional notation pieces?

"THE WONDER WHEEL"

MASTY: Jon, I have two ideas.

JON: Let's hear them.

MASTY: My parents and baby brother came to visit, and we went to an amusement park. I was afraid I wouldn't have time to come up with a piece for today, but when I was sitting in the park *two* pieces came to me in about five minutes!

JON: Remember, everyone, that great ideas are all around us. We just have to keep our eyes, ears, and noses on the alert. Masty, please continue.

MASTY: As I was sitting in the amusement park I was watching the Ferris wheel, with the passenger cars rotating around, and it struck me. What would it look and sound like to have notes rotating around on a music staff? So, here is my piece. I have been playing it as a solo piece. I think the piece looks pretty cool also.

JON: I remember from my childhood an incredibly huge Ferris wheel called The Wonder Wheel, in Coney Island in Brooklyn, New York.

MASTY: I was looking for a title for this piece. Can I call it "The Wonder Wheel"?

Fig. 3.1. "The Wonder Wheel"

MASTY: I kept it simple, using only four notes rotating. Each note represents a passenger car. I made each note a different shape so I could keep track of them.

JON: Good idea.

MASTY: I like the music, and I find a nice, even, clocklike tempo is most effective.

JON: That's great conceptual art thinking, using archetypes like circular machines, Ferris wheels, and clocks to inspire pitches and rhythm for your piece. Let's give a listen.

Masty plays her solo interpretation of "The Wonder Wheel."

MASTY: I enjoy the chromatic rotation of the motif. How can I develop it?

JON: One simple variation would be to play it backwards. Then the motif would spin counter-clockwise.

Masty jumps right in and tries reversing the motion.

JON: Masty has just shown us the improvisatory power of strong sight-reading, by being able to read her "Wonder Wheel" piece backwards!

"The Wonder Wheel" in Traditional Notation

JON: One important thing, class. By expanding our view of traditional notation, as Masty has done by using various-shaped note heads to help her follow the rotation motif, we can conceive of a development that would have been difficult to see in basic traditional notation. Then we can translate our new visions back into traditional notation. Here is "The Wonder Wheel" in traditional notation. Remember that one of the goals here in the workshop is to open up fresh creative resources for ourselves, and bring them back to an accessible form for use in our everyday playing and composing with others.

Fig. 3.2. "The Wonder Wheel" in Traditional Notation

Let's let Masty's beautiful "Wonder Wheel" graphic inspire some other artistic possibilities. As I look at Masty's graphic, I'm captivated by the four rotating graphic symbols, and I imagine, from a bird's-eye view, four dancers with four different hats of different colors moving in an interesting circular choreography, spinning slowly, dervishlike.

I can also imagine the four rotating graphic symbols as a moving motif for a mural or a quilt—the four symbols of different colors each tumbling along through their cycle.

The fascination of cycles as developmental motif is endless. Much has been written about cycles—life cycles, seasonal cycles, and the like—but what about using formal cycles in writing? How about a short story that begins mid-sentence and ends with the beginning of that sentence, so that the whole story is a great circle? (James Joyce's novel Finnegan's Wake does this.) What about a poem with a rotating rhyme scheme like this: abcd bcda cdab dabc abcd? There are many possibilities for using formal cycles in writing. The four seasons are inspired by cycles. Or is it the other way around?

"ROLLER COASTERS"

MASTY: Jon, here is another amusement park–inspired piece. This idea came from the roller coaster at the amusement park. I took a piece of manuscript paper and let my pencil produce roller coaster–like shapes along the staff. A player follows the line and plays the notes that the line moves through. Each player will interpret it differently, of course. The lines should be played as quickly as possible at times. It *is* a roller coaster!

JON: Wow, Masty, you should be directing this class. These are great ideas. Please pass out the music and conduct the workshop yourself. You *are* the composer.

Masty jumps right up to direct the ensemble.

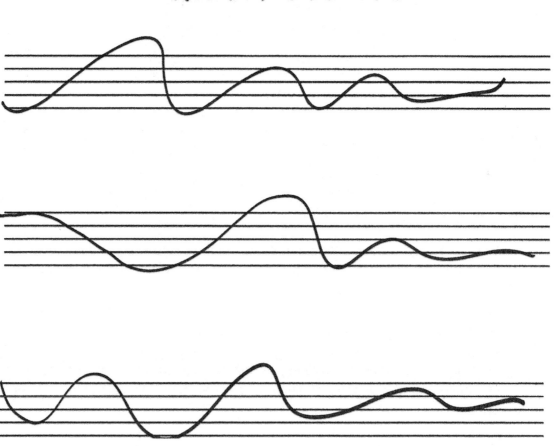

Fig. 3.3. "Roller Coasters"

MASTY: Let's play the first roller coaster line together.

EZRA: You mean roughly together? You said yourself that each of us would interpret the lines differently.

MASTY: Thanks Ezra, you're right. Try at least to begin and end the line together. When the line goes uphill, slow down, accelerate on the downhill sections.

Masty gives a cue and the workshop enthusiastically zips through the first roller coaster line.

MASTY: Now let's play the second line.

CreW again zips along nicely.

MASTY: Jon, did I do the assignment correctly? Is this expanding traditional notation?

JON: You took the veritable spine of traditional notation language, the staff, and used it as a foundation. And the graphic image of the line gives a basic guide to the notes on the staff. I would say it is a good example of stretching things.

MASTY: I like the freedom that the roller coaster line gives to the players. How can I exert more control over pitches used but keep the rhythmic freedom?

JON: Here's a notation technique tailor-made for your request, which I call "proportional notation."

PROPORTIONAL NOTATION

JON: Proportional notation is a close relative of traditional notation. In proportional notation, traditional note heads are used to indicate pitches on the staff, but instead of flags and beams to indicate the duration of notes, as in traditional notation, a note's duration is indicated by its proportional visual distance from the next note. The top horizontal line indicates the sounding of the pitch, and the line's absence indicates silence. I'll sketch on the whiteboard the first line of "Roller Coasters" written in proportional notation.

Fig. 3.4. "Roller Coasters," First Line in Proportional Notation

JON: The composer can indicate a speed, or tempo, by stating, as I have done, one centimeter equals one second. Proportional notation is less "accurate" rhythmically than traditional notation, but enables the rhythms to breathe more in the hands of the performer, and this is what Masty wants in this piece.

MASTY: Thanks, Jon.

JON: You're welcome, Masty.

Proportional notation looks rather beautiful, fanlike. What would it look like, and sound like, if we applied these proportional notation concepts to writing and reading the words of a story or a poem to indicate reading speed and how loudly or softly the text should be read? It may be difficult to read. What do you think? I think it may simply take a bit of getting used to. The bigger the letters, the louder you get, and the farther apart the words are, the slower you read. Get it?

Right now I   am   be gin   ning
to   ge   t   Slee   eeee   py   I
need   some   rest

Teachers, actors, broadcasters, and others who use their voices for a living have to learn to exaggerate the natural pitch variations in their voices. As vocal coaches will tell you, people in their ordinary, everyday speaking voice tend to vary their pitches too little, and to speak within a range that is uncomfortably high. By learning to lower the middle of our range and to vary our pitch around that middle, we can produce a speaking voice that is much more pleasant and musical to listen to. As a way of training oneself to do this, write down some text using vertical placement of the words to indicate register. So, a broadcaster might say,

that's
        the   Tues-   March eigh-
            way   day   2000 and
and   it   teenth
                        was
                                        10.

Musicians could try the above speech exaggerations with their melodic ideas, expanding their interval- and direction-playing possibilities.

Painting a cool-looking humongous minimalist mural with clean black vertical lines spaced for a feeling of movement along the canvas might be interesting.

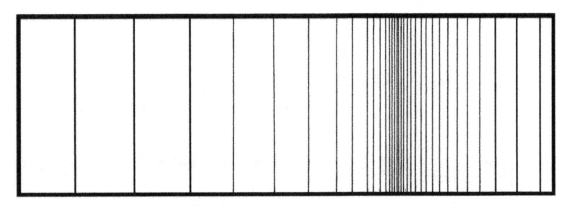

Fig. 3.5. Mural

CHESTER: Jon, you mentioned the term "canon" a little earlier today. Can you define what a canon is? I've heard of it in music. You said that the technique is also used in choreography.

JON: A canon is essentially a round. The traditional song "Frère Jacques" is an example of a round, as is "Three Blind Mice."

CHESTER: Do you mean when a song begins and then another voice begins the same song a little later as an accompaniment?

JON: Yes. The repetition overlaps with the original. Imitation such as this is a very powerful compositional device that gives a diagonal strength, and is essentially timeless. As you may notice, I love using canon technique with CreW. Another piece, anyone?

"FOR KEN J. ROMERE"

ROBERTO: Jon, I took you literally when you said last week that we could cut and hybridize traditional notation materials. Can you take a look at what I did with "Yesterdays?" I hope Jerome Kern isn't looking. I created a collage with the tune.

JON: That's right, Roberto, you mentioned that you were also a visual artist as well as a cook in our first meeting during introductions. Please proceed.

ROBERTO: I took a photocopy of Jerome Kern's "Yesterdays" and cut it into individual bars. Then I pieced the bars together in another order that I felt worked musically. I added a note here and there to help rhythmic momentum. Can I play it for the class as a solo piece?

JON: Sure, and it's also a nice concept visually.

ROBERTO: I call it "For Ken J. Romere."

Fig. 3.6. "For Ken J. Romere"

JON: That sounds sweet, Roberto. Very Duke Ellington-ish. It's powerful how the original motifs of "Yesterdays" play peek-a-boo, which is the magical effect of a collage. And your title "For Ken J. Romere"—is this piece written for a friend?

ROBERTO: No, it's a collage using the letters of the name "Jerome Kern," the composer of "Yesterdays."

JON: Nice idea.

YUTO'S "COLLAGE STUDY"

YUTO: I have a piece I wrote for a friend whose family is being torn apart by a divorce. I felt sad for him and I created this piece to express my feelings. I took some music and tore it into small, randomly sized pieces and created a collage, like Roberto did, except I put this together very freely. Can I show it to the class?

Fig. 3.7. Yuto's "Collage Study"

JON: Wow, that looks really beautiful.

YUTO: Thank you. I hope it will capture and express my friend's confusion and sadness. I would like each member of the ensemble to look at the image and play the visual path that his or her eyes naturally take through the page. Try not to make the playing sound forced. After a while, I would like Jon to conduct strong, short attacks with silence in between, and then one final sustained chord.

JON: Yuto, come up and conduct this yourself. I'll play your part.

Yuto gives a cue to start things off, gives some very dramatic conducting motions for the strong, staccato attacks, and then cues the final chord.

JON: Wow—that final chord is incredibly beautiful. CreW, please play that last chord again on cue. Okay, play. . . nice. Please write down exactly the notes you just played. We will discuss it in a moment. Yuto, your piece is a wonderful artistic effort. You're expressing visually the confusion and sadness your friend is having, and using visual art and music art as powerful mediums here. It's interesting that you and Roberto, both visual artists, are using collage technique for your pieces. I remember in art school I was assigned to do a collage to help see one possible visual transition to modern abstract art technique.

The workshop has been creating music with collage technique and canon technique. Both of these terms and techniques are also used in choreography. Collage is a dance form that consists of movements, often with no connection, that are done together. As mentioned earlier, canon in dance is a particular movement reflected by different dancers at different times. Bring both of these techniques into your medium. Another music term, "beats," is used in acting for timing and emotions.

Creative Workshop ideas such as Yuto's fresh approach with his collage bring players into the moment, inspired to truly improvise, to take a fresh, mysterious path of possibilities with no restrictive dictates connected to it.

EZRA'S HAIKU VARIATION IDEA

EZRA: Jon, an idea just struck me. As you know from our introductions on the first day of the workshop, I'm also a poet, and I loved the haiku "Old Pond" by the master Bashō that Yuto brought in last week. I'm also inspired by the collage technique Roberto and Yuto used today, and would like to try creating variations of "Old Pond" by cutting up the haiku into separate words and finding new haikus. I hope that's not being disrespectful, Yuto.

YUTO: Don't worry, Bashō will not get angry. He has been dead for more than 400 years!

EZRA: Great. I'll bring in some possibilities next week.

JON: Thank you, Ezra. Now, CreW please take out the "Democratic Chorale" we started last week. How many chords did we vote on and sketch down so far?"

CREW: Three.

JON: OK. Leave some room after the already written notes of the "Democratic Chorale" and write down the notes you just played for the last chord of Yuto's piece. We will make this the last chord of the chorale. Please put "Democratic Chorale" away in your folders. We will continue filling in the rest of the chords later.

> In his wonderful book *Notations*, John Cage compiled music works that explore how various composers have stretched and sculpted with the traditional notation language to produce scores that have become beautiful visual art pieces in themselves. Check out George Crumb's "Black Angels."

AN EXPANDING NOTATION OPUS FROM YESTERYEAR

JON: Every year for Valentine's Day, my very sweet wife, Betsy, makes me a beautiful shirt. We go to the fabric store and pick out some material for the shirt. One year we found material that was a display of traditional notation symbols—notes, clefs, and accidentals swirling in the fabric, freely, with no staffs. I was fascinated with the images, so I photocopied various parts of my new shirt, one for each player. I also gave each player a clear plastic sheet with staff paper copied onto it. I had each player place the sheeting over the copies of the shirt and read a section of the music. Well, as best they could. Here is a bit of the left shoulder.

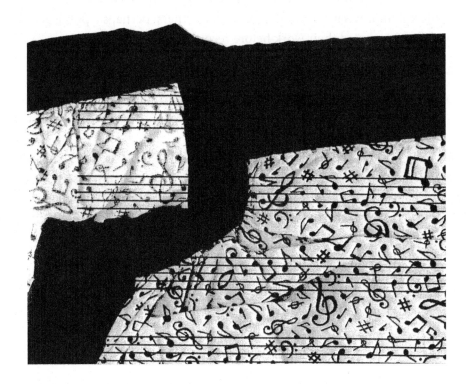

Fig. 3.8. Jon's Expanding Notation Opus from Yesteryear

> Readers, I hope you are enjoying the fun I'm having sharing CreW ideas with you. It's fun to let the imagination take over, which is what *Fresh Music* is all about!

OUR FAVORITE COMPOSER THEME

JON: As we have seen over the past few weeks, CreW is a nice place to work on our improvisation and composition technique. And what better way is there to study *comprovisation,* as I like to call it, than with our favorite composers.

BRUNO: But Jon, aren't many of them like, kinda . . . dead?

JON: You're right. I guess you can say they're *de*composing!

Light laughter drifts through the workshop.

JON: I don't actually mean studying with a composer personally, but rather through their music and with *your* help.

CHESTER: How can we study improvisation with these composers? They weren't improvisers. They wrote everything down.

JON: Remember, Chester, last week when we were discussing sight-reading and I mentioned that all written music was first an idea in one's mind. Then the idea was realized on an instrument to expand (improvise) on the idea's possibilities. At the moment of final acceptance of these possibilities, the comproviser wrote the ideas down on a piece of music paper to remember that wonderful improvisation and to pass it on to others, perhaps a publisher. This was how composers documented their work before recording technology.

INTRODUCTION: "AIR ON THE G STRING"

JON: For our Favorite Composer theme, I would like you to share a favorite composer with the workshop. Help the rest of CreW to experience and learn about your composer's techniques through verbal description, actual notated music of the composer, or a combination of these. If you wish, bring in a recording of the composer's work and have the workshop work from an aural stimulus. Right now I would like to share two of my favorite composers with you. Let's go to the later years of the Baroque period and look at the first section of Johann Sebastian Bach's "Air on the G String."

Aria (Air on the G String)

J.S. Bach

Fig. 3.9. "Air on the G String"

JON: I have produced a bare bones version for simplicity's sake. The top staff is the theme and the bottom staff is a simple quarter-note accompaniment. I have also included chord symbols as a guide for improvisation.

TIM: Isn't that weird to have chord symbols on a piece of classical music?

JON: Not really. Figured bass, an accompaniment language used during the Baroque period—and even today in certain music circles—is essentially chord symbols. The challenge here is to play the theme and its accompaniment, to play an improvisation that maintains the magic of Bach's music. I personally find this difficult, and feel it is like handling fine china or crystal—one awkward note, or inflection, shatters the phrase, the ambience. Study how Bach works with the tonalities, his approach tones, and the interval relationships. Steal from him. For now, let's play the written material just once as an inspiration for the improvisations that we will try next week. Slowly . . . *three and four and . . .*

EZRA: Beautiful!

JON: Yes it is, Ezra. And how the melody builds in intensity and returns to rest—a great example of control of cadence. Please study the theme and its accompaniment. We'll work on developing and improvising with "Air on the G String" at our next meeting.

"BÉLA BARTÓK SKETCHES"

JON: Here is a look at another of my favorite composers, Béla Bartók. I will share his musical prowess with you in a different way. I have brought in a recording of Bartók's *Concerto for Orchestra*. I will play only the first three minutes, and I would like you to describe the music you are hearing, in real time, using any combination of words or notes and/or simple sketches, so you can then later play from your descriptions. This is simply a reflection of Bartók's work, and will not sound like the original; that is not the intention here. This is just one of my ideas about how to share Bartók's music with you and create some nice new pieces of music. Please grab your pencils and paper.

I play the Bartók excerpt and the class sketches down their ideas. After about three minutes there's a request.

ROBERTO: Jon, please play it another time.

JON: Okay. Class, one more time.

I play the excerpt again.

JON: Now, let's take a look at your work. In fact, trade your sketches with your neighbor. You will be amazed how differently each person will translate the music he or she heard. As I glance at your work, some folks have used graphic images, arrows, and squiggly lines on plain paper, and some have sketched actual notes on manuscript paper *along* with words and graphic images. Find your own interpretation again, and now each of you play a solo statement working from your description. Bruno, let's begin from your end of the room.

Each workshop member plays his or her solo interpretation, and some very nice musical statements emerge.

JON: Today you have listened to Bartók's music, notated the experience in words, symbols, and notes, and then interpreted it again with music; what a nice cycle.

Join in here and try the Béla Bartók Sketches technique. Use any piece of music. Play only one to two minutes of it, and then write a basic description of the music in simple words, and/or describe it with a simple sketch. Reflect this description in your art medium. How about as a caricature? A 10-x-12-foot mural? A short story?

ASSIGNMENT FOR WEEK 4

JON: To close up for this week, I'd like to congratulate you on some wonderful expansions of traditional notation pieces. We actually played five world premieres today! I look forward to hearing about your favorite composers next week. How you would like to share your favorite composer is up to you.

I hope, my fellow artists, that you are getting ideas for your own new works, your own premieres. I have always liked to think our job as artists is to transform the stagnant bottoms of society's barrels of non-love and tired thinking by bringing forth fresh ideas filled with love to show the world that hope and infinity still exist.

Here is one of my favorite uses of language ideas brought into the workshop. It consists of a simple sentence. Try it, please.

"Play the most beautiful melody that you've never heard before as being played by someone you've never met before."

Or . . .

"Paint the most beautiful painting that you've never seen before as being painted by someone you've never met before."

Or . . .

"Dance the most beautiful dance that you've never seen before as being danced by someone you've never met before."

Of course this can go on and on! What I like best is that if you don't like what you produced from this idea you can blame it on that someone you've never met before!

CHAPTER 4 – WEEK 4
OUR FAVORITE COMPOSERS

You can observe a lot just by watching. —Yogi Berra

EZRA'S HAIKU COLLAGE ATTEMPTS

Ezra excitedly raises his hand.

EZRA: Would everyone like to hear the two haiku variations I created from Bashō's "Old Pond" using collage technique?

JON: Of course Ezra, can you sketch them on the whiteboard?

Ezra writes:

A pond
Sound jumps
The old water frog

The old water jumps
A pond
Frog sound

EZRA: How do they look and sound, Yuto?

YUTO: Fine. I must tell you that they are not official, traditional haiku, which has three lines and a strict number of syllables in each line: five, seven, five.

EZRA: Yikes! You're right. The English translation doesn't have enough syllables!

YUTO: But don't worry, we are here to explore and I think your variations have a certain charm to them.

EZRA: You are kind to say that.

I offer some honest encouragement.

JON: Ezra, your collage approach to creating haiku is very good. I think it's a wonderful start.

EZRA: Thanks, Jon.

JON: CreW, I look forward to learning about some of your favorite composers today.

TIM: Is it okay to show an expanding traditional notation piece before we explore the composer theme?

JON: Sure. And remember, CreW, when an inspiration comes to you, let us know right away.

"The Alphabet Tune": Tim's Expanding Traditional Notation Assignment

TIM: I remember you mentioning that with practice, our music sight-reading language ability will become as fluent as our language reading and writing abilities. So I combined the two languages by sketching the letters of the alphabet on the music staff, with notes, and I found some very interesting melodic and harmonic possibilities. My only problem is, now what? Here is my work so far.

Fig. 4.1. "The Alphabet Tune"

JON: This piece certainly does look interesting, Tim. Since I see some vertical chord shapes here, and you play guitar, can you play some of these letters for us?

TIM: I'll try. Some of them are tricky.

Tim plays the letter A and the letter B and struggles a bit with the letter C.

TIM: So now what do we do with these letter motifs?

JON: Since they're letters, spell something easy like *C-A-T*, cat.

Tim musically "spells" out cat.

TIM: Should we do a whole sentence now?

JON: Let's think in more simple terms, since we're searching for an "over-all" form to build upon. Let's try a "simple song form" that is expressed with letters: AABA form. Let's give the rest of CreW a chance to play some of these letters and the musical motifs they create. If you don't play a harmonic instrument, play the notes as a melody moving in the order you would use to write the letter. The letter motifs Tim has drawn are the "under-all" forms for this piece. Roberto, you play the letter A, and Masty, you play the letter B of the AABA form.

Roberto and Masty slowly work out their letters and play them.

JON: As you can see, the simple magic of song form, repetition, contrast, and return is at work here. Now we can try another form, rondo, or pyramid form, ABCDCBA. Ezra, you play letter C, and Yuto, play letter D. Start if off, Roberto. Now we're getting somewhere.

TIM: Jon, I have a cool idea. Let's use ABRACADABRA form!

JON: That's right, Tim, you mentioned your love for magic during our first week's introductions. And it does sound like an interesting form, with elements of repetition and return, and a couple of surprises thrown in. Magical. And Tim, please come up and cue each letter for us. Chester, play the letter R, and Bruno, you set up some magical ambiance.

Tim cues Bruno and then cues the letters. Tim makes three passes through the ABRACA-DABRA form, occasionally speeding up, followed by a ritardando, a slowing down, for the ending.

JON: Nice job, CreW, and thanks, Tim. This piece was a perfect introduction to the terms "under-all" and "over-all" form, which we will discuss later. The piece is also a perfect use of language to inspire our music.

An interesting note: the expression "abracadabra" has a number of possible derivations, one of which is from Hebrew, meaning "I create what I speak."

I am a big fan of drawing inspiration from language, and Tim's use of the alphabet is one of my favorite language pieces both visually and musically. Letters are effective in displaying a musical form, as you can see in the previous workshop dialogue. The letters are used simply as a basic guide—no details, simply when and where an idea is stated, if it is repeated, and when and where new ideas enter. This technique would work for taking a fresh look at the development of any performance, visual, or literary art form. In fact, the classic song form AABA and its representation of the classic pattern of repetition (rhythm) and contrast kindles memories of my visual art composition classes. "Repetition and contrast" was my art instructor's favorite "chant."

OUR FAVORITE COMPOSER THEME
JON'S BEETHOVEN DREAM

JON: Before we warm up with Johann Sebastian Bach's "Air on the G String," I'd like to share something with you. It must have been guilt about putting chord symbols to Bach's music that precipitated a crazy but illuminating dream I had the other night.

CREW: Was it scary Jon?

JON: You guys can be the judge. Dreams seem to "evaporate" quickly after you wake up, but this one really stayed with me for some reason.

In my dream it was a rainy day. An impressive-looking gentleman stood across from Berklee College, in front of an old stone church. He was well dressed, had a full face with longish hair, and seemed very familiar. Curious, I crossed the street, and lo and behold, it was Ludwig van Beethoven! I excitedly let out a greeting.

"Good day, Mr. Beethoven."

"Good morning, lad," he replied. His eyes focused on the instrument on my back. "What is that on your back that makes you look so turtlelike?"

"That's my guitar," I replied.

"I am also a musician and composer," he said. "I would love to hear you play something."

I nervously extracted my instrument from its case and proceeded to play a favorite standard, harmonized its melody, and began to improvise a solo for about sixteen bars when he abruptly interrupted me.

"That initial theme you played was lovely," he said, "but what are you playing right now?"

"That's my improvisation," I said proudly.

Beethoven replied, "I dabble in improvisation myself, usually to work developmental ideas into a composition. What are you improvising with?"

I pulled out my fake book and pointed to the chord symbols of the standard I had just played. "I am working from these chord symbols."

Glancing at the music, he asked, "Are these symbols similar to figured bass, the harmonic language used in classical music?"

"Yes," I said, "they are similar in that they indicate a particular harmonic progression to be used for accompaniment."

Beethoven responded skeptically, "Why would you base your improvisation primarily on accompaniment material? I was wondering why your improvisation sounded so lost after hearing your wonderful playing of the theme."

I mumbled, "Well, I . . ."

He interrupted, asking, "May I play something for you?"

I led the way into the school, and to a room with a piano. He immediately began playing a very impressive piece, which he commented on in a running dialogue. "Now listen to how I state a theme. Then I develop or improvise on it by taking some of the theme and putting it in the bottom of these chord structures. Now the theme is inverted." He continued in this way until the end of the piece.

"Bravo," I stammered.

"Why, thank you," he said. "I feel it's more efficient to use the energy of the principal theme's personality in developing the piece rather than continually introducing new themes, as it seemed you did during your performance. It also strengthens my composition as a whole."

"Wow!" I replied, and immediately awoke from my dream.

> My Beethoven dream was a lesson in efficiency. Maintain a focus on a subject, a theme, draw new ideas and energy from it, and see an infinity of possibilities. Place a theme in a new light, like the impressionist painters who did this literally—for instance, Monet, who painted Rouen Cathedral at various times of day in different light.
>
> I remember clearly, during a museum trip, viewing the many preliminary sketches—thumbnails of a subject, a theme—that an artist would produce to help adjust and compose the theme before beginning the grand finale, the last statement. In one series Picasso produced 200 drawings of the same female subject, beginning with a complete drawing, and with each subsequent sketch removing elements, ending with a final sketch consisting of a few essential lines. This is a good example of developing material through the technique of extraction.

JON: After my Beethoven dream, I lay there in bed in a labored sweat and realized how inefficient I was in my composing and improvisation, rarely drawing upon a tune's melody, the primary theme for creative material. So let's try Bach's "Air on the G String," but let's try not to rely only on those chord symbols. I don't want to have that dream again! Let's see if we can draw our ideas from the melodic and harmonic motifs.

"AIR ON THE G STRING"

JON: Today let's focus on the first twelve bars that we played last week and really work from the melodic motifs. Grab the music out of your folders, folks. Are there any thoughts about how you will approach the development section, your improvisations, in this piece?

Fig. 4.2. "Air on the G String"

BRUNO: Jon, I noticed Bach often likes to begin a measure on a basic chord tone relative to the accompanying chords.

JON: Good observation, Bruno. The basic chord tone sets a tonal quality quickly and gives something to build on.

TIM: I noticed that simple approach notes to the basic chord tones work nicely also, as Bach uses in the sixth and eighth bars. I also notice that when I try that, it doesn't sound as nice.

JON: There's a lot more going on here than meets our analytical eye. At this point I'm beginning to see the piece as one simple melody that changes every two bars, and with transitional material like arpeggios, with approach notes connecting the simple melodic line. Bach seems to have an uncanny sense of musical smell. Let's try this, just these first twelve bars. We will state the theme, and then improvise on those twelve bars working with Bach's melodic ideas.

Refer to the chord symbols as needed. Yuto, please be the first soloist, then Chester, Tim, and so forth. Slowly now . . . *three and four.*

The workshop has its moments, some delicate ones.

BRUNO: I don't feel like I should be improvising to Johann Sebastian Bach. It seems like sacred ground or something.

JON: I know how you feel, Bruno. I feel the same way. It's still fun to try. I'm sure that Bach didn't like all of his ideas enough to write them down.

So who would like to share another composer with us?

> Challenging ourselves by trying to replicate the masters is nothing new for forward-thinking music and art students such as ourselves. Museums are always speckled with sketching art students trying to glean some technique from the masterworks on exhibit.

"A POTPOURRI OF DEBUSSY"

ROBERTO: About two weeks ago in my history of music class, we listened to Claude Debussy's String Quartet no. 1, his only string quartet, and I really loved the music. Then I went to the library and listened to some of his orchestral pieces, and they were wonderful also. Since he has been my favorite composer, at least for the past two weeks, I did some research and voilà! I have a piece, which is part mine and part Debussy's.

JON: Sounds good so far, Roberto.

ROBERTO: During my Debussy research, I came across a term, "pandiatonicism," a technique used by Debussy. From what I can tell, the term refers to modal music, using the notes of a diatonic scale, but using them without purposefully maintaining a particular tonal center.

JON: In other words, all the tones of the diatonic scale are equal?

ROBERTO: Yes, that's a simple way to say it. I found this really cool book in the library titled *A Dictionary of Musical Themes.* The book gives just the first several bars of more than 10,000 themes, from Albeniz to Zimbalist. I looked up Debussy and sketched down tantalizing bits of his themes. I transposed them all to the same key, and thought it would be fun to hear what a pandiatonic "Potpourri of Debussy" would sound like.

JON: Should we play all the themes together?

ROBERTO: We can play one theme and try some canons with it, or play all the themes together? There are many possibilities.

JON: May we see the music, mon ami?

ROBERTO: Oui, Jean.

A Potpourri of Debussy

Fig. 4.3. "A Potpourri of Debussy"

JON: Please direct us, Roberto.

ROBERTO: Okay. Let's dive right in and hear all the themes together. Chester, play theme one, Masty, theme two, and right across the room. Jon, please play theme eight. Not too slowly everyone.

Roberto counts off. CreW plays for a bit. Roberto stops the ensemble.

ROBERTO: Since Debussy was an impressionist and a pioneer in creating new orchestral colors, like his impressionist colleagues in the visual arts created color variations of a single subject, please explore a range of tone colors when playing these various themes. Chester, you start first and repeat your theme, and try varying the tone color. Masty, you enter with your theme after two bars of Chester's theme, and repeat your theme. Continue with those regular entrances until we're all playing together. Then let's get really soft and muted, and have some nice open solos above this tonal texture. Then let's play all the themes once for an ending. Is that clear? The same tempo *and three, four* . . .

CreW really plays well.

ROBERTO: Sorry for my humility, but I really liked that.

TIM: This theme six sounds a lot like "God Save the King."

ROBERTO: Yes, in one of Debussy's preludes he uses quodlibet and creates a parody of "God Save the King." He opens the piece with the "God Save the King" melody, simply stated, but with powerful harmonies supporting the melodic line.

Ezra's hand shoots up.

EZRA'S "TONE MAZE"

EZRA: Is it okay to do another Bach piece? I love his music also.

JON: Of course, go right ahead.

EZRA: This is a combination of story form, expanding traditional notation, and favorite composer theme all rolled into one.

JON: Remember that an important function of the ideas expressed in CreW is that they become catalysts, sparks for your creative work. It's fine to combine techniques. Please continue, Ezra.

EZRA: As I was on a break from practicing my reading with some of Bach's minuets, which are dance pieces, I was silently looking at the music and imagining the page of music as a ballroom floor with dancers moving across it. So I drew possible paths for various dancers on the music sheet, the conceptual dance floor. It ended up looking like a maze, so I call the piece "The Tone Maze." Here is my sketch.

Fig. 4.4. "The Tone Maze"

JON: This looks great, Ezra.

EZRA: I've made seven different dancer's paths. Some meet up with other paths. Each of us starts on an assigned path and continues to the goal in the right bottom corner. Roberto, take path one, Masty path two, I will take three, Yuto four, Chester, Tim, and Bruno paths five, six, and seven.

JON: Should all paths be played at one time?

EZRA: Yes, and when you come to the goal at the end of a path, stop playing.

JON: Should we keep an even, minuet-like dance tempo?

EZRA: Let's play two variations, one in a free tempo and one stating an even, dancelike tempo.

After Ezra's cue the first variation took barely forty-five seconds as each player moved through the maze to the goal.

EZRA: Now let's try it in minuet or waltz tempo. Ready? One bar outside, not too fast, *one, two, three . . .*

The in-tempo version took a little more time.

JON: Any comments, Ezra?

EZRA: I like the effects in both but wish it could last longer.

MASTY: You can have the *dancers* repeat their paths again if you wish, or have each player move to the next numbered path after their first path is complete. At the end of the seven-path cycle each player plays their original path for a final statement.

JON: Thanks, Masty. This piece is a nice addition to our repertoire. Thank you, Ezra.

Ezra's concept—imagining dancers moving through one of Bach's minuets creating various paths through the sheet music (dance floor)—is quite beautiful. What is special about Ezra's piece is that it sets the players quite literally on a new path of possibility. No room for ego and showing off chops here. It would be interesting, and probably very expensive, to actually do this as a choreography. There's a stairway at the Museum of Science in Boston whose stairs produce specific tones when stepped upon. How about a maze built on a ballroom floor, with sound triggers along the paths of the maze? The dancers would create a fascinating piece of music as they danced their paths through the maze.

"BEBOP SPEEDWAY"

JON: Any more composer-inspired pieces?

BRUNO: Here's an idea that taps into my favorite jazz composer, Charlie "Yardbird" Parker. I call this "Bebop Speedway." I have heard about those "cutting sessions" the early beboppers would have. Players would try to blow each other off the bandstand with hot licks, calling tunes in challenging keys and dropping cymbals in the middle of someone's solo. I thought, what's more intensely cutting and competitive than a roaring speedway? So I found seven Charlie Parker blues compositions, one for each player—"Air Conditioning," "Now's the Time," "Au Privave," "Bluebird," etc.—and I would like us to play the heads as fast as possible, and at the same time. It should have the intensity of a racetrack.

CreW liked the idea, but some were concerned that they couldn't read music well enough to handle the task.

BRUNO: OK, let's play "Bebop Speedway" next week after we have a chance to get these blues heads up to racetrack speed. We need to have someone who wins the race, and they can play a victory chorus, perhaps a solo on their blues head.

JON: Great ideas, Bruno.

BRUNO: Here are the lead sheets. Just pick one that seems okay. Or pick a Parker blues of your own to use. Any key is fine. I don't want a pandiatonic atmosphere. It is really the intensity that I'm looking for.

JON: Bruno, it sounds like you want a pantonal atmosphere in which all tonalities are fine. It's nice to have some bebop in our repertoire.

I have a favorite composer idea that I hope will work.

A JOHN CAGE STUDY WITH PREPARED INSTRUMENTS

JON: John Cage was an American composer who did early work with chance music, electronic music and prepared instruments. The term "prepared" simply means that an instrument is altered physically from its original state. Detuning a string instrument randomly is a start. Placing objects in an instrument, such as the strings of a piano, to change the delivery of its mechanisms is another. These preparations can be very detailed or not, depending on a composer's intentions. Class, I would like each of you to clear your music stand for a moment and empty your pockets onto it.

Clinking and rummaging sounds result and small piles of coins, keys, cell phones, pieces of paper, cards, and other objects appear.

JON: Now take any of these objects and gently prepare your instruments by sticking objects in the bell of your instrument, or between your instrument's strings and fingerboard. Remember, your ego will be having a tough time playing in these strange Cagean preparations since you will be getting a totally different response from your instrument. Hopefully, by this, our fourth week as CreWsters, you will be fairly accepting of unusual sounds. Now that our instruments are prepared, I have some simple ideas I would like to try. But first let's hear some of the sounds you're getting.

The workshop tries their "new" instruments for a moment with mixed results.

JON: In the world of avant garde music everything sounds good.

TIM: Is that a good thing?

JON: I certainly think so. That much more beauty in life.

First let's imagine that we are a giant wind chime, each of us a strand of the chime as it moves in the wind. My hand will conduct the wind's motion. As I sweep my hand by you, activate your part of the wind chime. As the wind leaves, you stop playing. My other hand will be directing dynamics. Ready? Here we go.

I direct with both hands and arms whirling dervishlike and enjoy directing this prepared workshop. After about ten minutes of explorations I slow down and conduct a final quick sweep of wind through the workshop.

JON: How did that go, folks?

TIM: I liked it!

CHESTER: You were right. It *is* taking me some time to get used to these new sounds coming out of my instrument.

JON: You can adjust them as you wish.

MASTY: Can we try something, Jon?

JON: Sure.

MASTY: Let's see how much we can rhythmically stay together. Can we play a rhythm all together? Let's try the rhythm of a tune that we all know. How about something simple, like "Frère Jacques." Let's play it twice for now. Here is a count . . . *one, two. . .*

The workshop plays remarkably well together, and after two times through, ends together.

MASTY: Thanks, Jon, that was awesome!

JON: Yes, it was, Masty. Controlled and out of control at the same time. Organized chaos. Lovely.

"HAPPY BIRTHDAY RUBBERTELLIE"

JON: I actually have a piece that I composed for prepared performer.

BRUNO: Sounds scary.

JON: The piece is called "Happy Birthday Rubbertellie," and it uses a very simple melody, the "Happy Birthday" theme. The birthday theme is played passacaglia-like, a series of variations on a theme. First the birthday theme is played simply. Then each subsequent variation of the birthday theme is created by playing the theme, but with a particular preparation of my body with an object such as a blindfold, a pair of handcuffs, hockey gloves, a straitjacket, and even a body bag for the finale!

EZRA: That sounds wild. I want to hear and see that. I've heard about your Rubbertellie, Jon. What exactly is it?

JON: The Rubbertellie is basically a standard guitar, but not held or tuned in a standard way, creating a totally new approach that opens up music possibilities that the standard guitar would not have offered me. I'll bring in a video titled *Heavy Rubber* and show it to the class. It's a documentary film that looks at thirty years of Rubbertellie's life. The film has "Happy Birthday Rubbertellie" in it.

Readers, for your interest, there is a photo of the Rubbertellie in action on the back cover.

Let's try preparing some of you visual artists. No, I don't mean as drastically as the "Happy Birthday Rubbertellie" opus just described. Let's start off simply with having you hold that paintbrush, or pencil, or chisel, in your weak hand while you work. Singers, and actors, throw some cotton balls in those cheeks, and try delivering some lines. Playing with your voice can open up some groundbreaking possibilities. Dancers, grab those ski boots and try some moves. In the seeming limitations some new possibilities will emerge.

Painters, how about grabbing a brush with your teeth, or your toes, and giving it a try. In these "prepared" physical states, a sense of freedom exists, freedom with no expectations, with no shoulds or coulds. You'll be perfectly fresh at it!

TUNE ROWS—"A TUNE ROW STUDY"

JON: Here's another favorite composer idea that uses quodlibet. In fact, in this composition technique I brazenly steal a tune's entire melody, and I'll never get caught!

I must thank the composer Arnold Schoenberg and his "tone row" concept for inspiring my concept for Tune Rows. The foundation of Mr. Schoenberg's tone row concept is to compose working from a series of tones consisting of all twelve notes of the chromatic scale with *no* repetition of notes.

CHESTER: That would sound strange.

JON: To some folks it does sound strange. Remember that beauty is in the ear (eye) of the beholder.

Here is the tone row Arnold Schoenberg used as a foundation for his Suite for Piano, op. 25.

E F G Db Gb Eb Ab D B C A Bb

The composer would build his composition by cycling through this *exact* order of tones, shaping the tones rhythmically, in various directions, piling some tones harmonically, and adding articulations, dynamics, and expression markings that suited his fancy as his composition unfolded. My Tune Row concept works with a series of tones, and a composition is created by cycling through this exact order of notes. The main difference is that with Tune Rows, the order of the notes is produced by stealing. Yes, I said pilfering, burglarizing, confiscating, shoplifting an already existing melody. "What!?" you may say, "but that's illegal and you could go to jail!" The key is to not get caught!

Remember that only the order of the notes is "borrowed," not the original groove, style, idiomatic language, rhythms, and directions of the tones. I have shared this composition technique with a number of folks, and the results have been impressive, especially in creating a momentum for someone going through "composing block."

Here's an example of Tune Rows technique in action. Can you guess the tune I am working from simply by listening to yourself playing it? If you are stumped, I put the answer right after the example in really small type! Don't cheat! This example goes twice through the original tune.

A Tune Row Study

Fig. 4.5. "A Tune Row Study"

(Happy Birthday)

A Look at Week 5
OVER-ALL FORMS

YUTO: How do some of these composers keep their ideas going for so long? I listened to that Bartók *Concerto for Orchestra*. It maintained a powerful sense of development throughout.

JON: Of course, Yuto, artistic genius is at work with these composers, as it is in our work here in CreW. As guideposts, composers work with over-all form to build their compositions just as we used Tim's idea for ABRACADABRA form for his "Alphabet Tune."

Since you have brought up this very important topic, we will work with over-all form some more next week.

A Workshop Consultation

JON: So class, and my dear readers and fellow artists, we have completed our fourth week of CreW. How are things going?

EZRA: I'm enjoying the class and learning about a lot of creative possibilities.

CHESTER: Some of my friends think we are doing wild things in here when they look at my folder.

JON: Remember that our everyday life is incredibly wild. We are so close up to it that we get used to it. Just imagine that we are in our studio painting or practicing, sculpting or working on an acting role, and just outside the window, a small, saucerlike spacecraft appears with two Saturnian-looking beings behind the wheel. What a fascinating sight we must be to these guys, with our brushes and canvases, instruments, and the sights and sounds we're making. Wow. Wild!

The creative explorations we are making here in CreW will help us to better appreciate the beautiful world all around us. And hopefully workshop ideas and techniques are helping you through any creative blocks you may stumble upon.

Music Theory Jargon for the Reader

Music is motion from nonrest to rest.   —Olivier Messiaen

Readers, I just had to use Olivier Messiaen's quote again. As you will see, it's a perfect fit here.

Before we begin week five of our workshop, an explanation of some musical terms like "chord symbol," and "II-V-I" ("two-five-one") is needed.

A chord symbol, such as C7, represents a chord, which is a group of music notes played at the same time. Chord symbols are connected to other chord symbols to create a chord progression, much like a word (a group of letters) is connected to other words to create a sentence. Chord progressions and sentences both have points of rest and points of nonrest. In chord progressions, Roman numerals are used to indicate rest and nonrest chords. For example, the Roman numeral I (one) indicates a rest chord. The Roman numerals II (two) and IV (four) and V (five) indicate types of nonrest chords. The II and IV chords are a medium level of nonrest, and the V chord is a high level of nonrest.

The following simple sentence moves from nonrest (Dick sees) to rest (Jane), much like the simple chord progression II-V (nonrest chords) moves to I (a rest chord).

(Nonrest) (rest)

Dick sees Jane

II V I

I hope that helps.

And one more note on the usefulness of learning music, including the music theory concepts in this book: In a recent TED-Ed Originals talk, Anita Collins and Sharon Colman Graham state that neuroscientists found that "those who were exposed to a period of music learning showed an enhancement in multiple brain areas compared to other activities including other arts." Here is the link: http://ed.ted.com/lessons/how-playing-an-instrument-benefits-your-brain-anita-collins

CHAPTER 5 – WEEK 5
FORM 101: OVER-ALL FORMS

Form is the balance between tension and relaxation. —Ernst Toch

A FORM-AL INTRODUCTION

JON: Good morning, CreW. Last week a question popped up: How do some of our favorite composers write compositions that last so long yet maintain interest? One of the key words here is composition. When was the first time we heard the word composition?

TIM: In English class, in grammar school.

MASTY: In art appreciation class.

JON: Yes. And what do writing composition, painting composition, and music composition all have in common?

MASTY: Stating and maintaining a central focus or theme, and how the artist develops the theme.

JON: Good, Masty. "Development" is another key word in this discussion, and it is how our composers build on "under-all" forms, or smaller forms, the microcosmic elements to create the over-all or larger form, the macrocosm of a piece.

BRUNO: What does the composer start with, the smaller forms or the big form? It sounds like the chicken or the egg conundrum.

JON: Great point, Bruno, and the word "point" happens to be another word for a theme or subject. How do you try to get a point, a theme, across to someone?

CHESTER: With some of my friends I have to keep repeating it a thousand times!

JON: Correct. Repetition is the perfect answer, and one of the key ingredients in today's subject, or theme, the word "form." In simple song form, AABA, the A repeats, then B appears, another section, a change or contrast, and then a return to A; so you have repetition, contrast, and return. I remember working in art school with repetition and contrast and return. Gastronomically speaking, not much different than chomping on some salty fries, taking a sip of a cool drink, then back to those fries. What a tasty cadence.

ABRACADABRA FORM REVISITED

JON: Forms come in all shapes and sizes. Last week, Tim's ABRACADABRA form was a wonderful addition to the menagerie of form possibilities, some of which we have used already. The words "canon," "minuet," "sonata," "fugue," "blues," and "rondo" are just a handful of terms having to do with form. And, of course, story form, which was the first form of the semester. Forms can be found everywhere—people-made forms, forms found in nature. Let's look at a simple under-all form for a moment, drawn from our traditional harmony lessons.

Readers, you may wish to review my brief music theory tutorial at the end of the last chapter. It will help with the following discussion.

EXPANDING CHORD SYMBOLS
THE II-V-I'S OF LIFE

JON: In our CreW communication explorations in week two, I introduced the "What Goes Up . . ." Study in which we observe when an idea comes to rest. I asked you what archery, sneezes, and bowling had in common. Let's talk about that again. Ezra?

EZRA: These activities build up tension, then release it.

JON: Right. In basic harmonic language, this building and releasing can be experienced in a simple II-V-I chord progression. We can say that archery, sneezing, and bowling are some II-V-I's of life, along with hundreds of other activities. Like Chester's wonderful-looking yawn and stretch.

CHESTER: Sorry, Jon, I had a late night.

JON: That's okay, Chester. Can anyone think of other II-V-I's of life?

CreW gives several enthusiastic responses:

"Jumping off a diving board."

"Simple sentences."

"Breathing."

JON: Those are great examples. With AABA form and Tim's ABRACADABRA form, letters are used to describe the *basic* chronology of a form. In a chord progression, the levels of rest and nonrest are described with Roman numerals. Let's look at archery again for a moment. In a II-V-I harmonic progression, the II chord has a medium level of nonrest, as in archery, just beginning to pull that bowstring back. The V chord has a high level of nonrest. Now the bowstring is pulled *way* back. Then the I chord, the release of the bowstring as it moves back to rest.

SPRECHT-BLOTS REVISITED

JON: Let's try Sprecht-Blots again just for a moment. Let's go through the workshop and improvise from each of these Sprecht-Blots. Each of these Sprecht-Blots I am speaking can be called II-V-I's of life.

JON: Bruno, please start us off and play your musical response to my first Sprecht-blot:

Snoring

Now Masty:

Swimming

JON: And let's continue around the workshop:

A sneeze
A toilet flush
A basketball foul shot
Eating sushi with wasabi

JON: Thanks, Roberto. It takes a while for that wasabi V chord to come to rest.

So each of these preceding Sprecht-Blots indicates a building in intensity and releasing, just like a II-V-I. How would you portray a II-V-I with three brush strokes, three ballet moves, three little words; a nice big yawn . . . A-HA! I GOTCHA!

Now that this chord stuff is hopefully making more "organic" sense to you, let's extend things.

BLUESSHAPE

JON: The terms "nonrest" and "rest" can also be thought of as "tension" and "relaxation"—as Ernst Toch says, "Form is the balance between tension and relaxation."

In music language, a II-V-I is an under-all form, a smaller part of the bigger picture, the over-all form. Let's expand our concept here to an over-all harmonic form, a good old 12-bar blues progression. With a concept I call "BluesShape," we can use the blues progression as a foundation, a form, to use with *anything in the universe*. With BluesShape we will use a basic 12-bar blues chord progression form that simply has a I chord (the resting chord), a IV chord (a nonresting chord) and a V chord (a really nonresting chord). Let's look at a blues progression in the key of C. I will write the twelve bars on the whiteboard. The progression has a more interesting array of movement from rest to nonrest than the more simple II-V-I progression. The blues progression also has that magical formula *repetition and contrast* built right into it.

Fig. 5.1. A 12-bar Blues Progression

JON: Just for fun, and to help us have a more expanded view of the blues progression, I am going to use my special seismo-harmonic analyzing pen here for a moment. It's really just a dry-erase marker. Just bear with my zaniness for a moment. I will move my special analyzing pen underneath the C7 blues progression. It will pick up the levels of rest and nonrest in the blues progression and display the reading as a seismographic-looking image. Notice how the V chord has a higher level of nonrest than the IV chord. That's important here. The final bar, the V chord, comes to rest to a I chord, the beginning of the next cycle of the progression. Here goes.

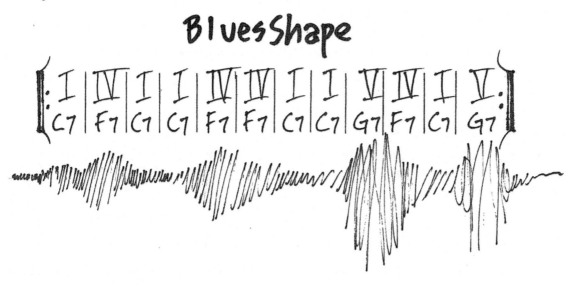

Fig. 5.2. BluesShape

MASTY: That looks pretty abstract to me!

JON: Yes it does, which is a good thing. It is interpreting the cadences of the blues progression chords into a graphic image that we can use as a visual form to inspire creative works using anything in the universe.

A SIMPLE BLUESSHAPE DANCE

JON: For our first look at using BluesShape, I would like you all to close your eyes and imagine that you are in the most beautiful theater in the world. You have front row seats. There is a solo dancer standing totally still on the stage. Do you all have this image?

Now, open your eyes. As I move my finger along and just below the BluesShape image, capture the BluesShape's image and levels of intensity with your dancer's movements. Ready? Let's try it slowly at first and just one time through. Here goes . . .

Reader, I hope your own imaginary dancer is trying this. Move along the BluesShape at an even pace with your eyes, and see how your own dancer responds.

JON: Okay, CreW, how was that first pass through?

ROBERTO: My dancer turned into a whirling dervish at one point, especially at the intense points.

JON: Good, Roberto.

YUTO: My dancer made very subtle motions. Perhaps my dancer will not be so shy on another pass through.

Light laughter lilts through the workshop.

JON: Thanks for sharing that, Yuto. Let's try that again, but now let's each hold up a hand, and that will now be your dancer. If you are inspired to, use both hands, two dancers. Two passes through the BluesShape this time, and a little faster. Here goes . . .

BLUESSHAPE FAUX TAI CHI

JON: Now, carefully place your instruments aside, and please stand up and spread out from your neighbor and your music stand. Get your whole body into the act and try some Faux Tai Chi to the BluesShape.

TIM: I've heard of Tai Chi before, but what is Faux Tai Chi?

JON: Faux is French for the word "false," so we're just faking some Tai Chi right now. I will join in here with you. Move at your own individual pace through the BluesShape. Let's go through the form several times.

> Now reader, get up outta that chair and Tai Chi, baby! This dancing stuff has a lot more to do with your medium than you may think. In fact, all fields of art have their own choreography. Film yourself working as an artist while painting, sculpting, teaching, parenting, cooking. For me they are all arts, and they each have their special dance. Does your dance reflect your love and connection to what you do?

CreW makes several Tai Chi passes following the BluesShape.

EZRA: That was fun and therapeutic, and I like how the movements from rest to nonrest seem to feel balanced.

JON: Good, Ezra. There is a proportion happening here in the blues progression. The highest intensity point, the V chord of the progression, occurs about two-thirds of the way through. This ratio is similar to Fibonacci ratio, a relative of the golden section.

TIM: We talked about golden section or golden means in math in high school. It's a division of something so that the whole is to the larger division as that division is to the smaller. It's supposed to produce a feeling of balance visually, and perhaps aurally, as in the case of BluesShape?

JON: Exactly, Tim. Thanks. For further study of golden section, take a look at *The Power of Limits: Proportional Harmonies in Nature, Art & Architecture* by Gyorgy Doczi.

A POLITICAL SPEECH USING BLUESSHAPE

BluesShape can be used as an inspiring form in any medium. The levels of intensity can be expressed as sound, visually, olfactorily, tactilely, in architecture as a series of buildings. And how about in a political speech?

Say, you wanna-be actors out there, give this political speech a try. I have labeled each line with a Roman numeral as a reference to the BluesShape form. Ride that BluesShape wave!

A Political Speech Using BluesShape

I

Good evening my fellow citizens. It is a pleasure to be here this evening

IV

and also to state a responsibility for both of us
to set the records straight in our country!

I

I come as your friend and fellow taxpayer

I

To meet you and begin working together

IV

To begin to create important, much-needed changes in our country!

IV

Changes that should have been made months ago!

I

Now we love our children, and their children,

I

Watching them grow is a pleasure.

V

But to see taxes foolishly spent, and not on our
children's educations, is an abomination!!

IV

And should be changed now!

I

to help our children's future.

V

A vote for me, and not for him is a vote in the right direction!!

I

Let's be friends and work together for our future.

MASTY: I'd vote for you, Jon.

JON: Thanks, Masty.

A BLUESSHAPE CHOIR

JON: Let's create some music together using BluesShape. Imagine we are the Tanglewood Festival Chorus. We will all sing together. Let's use some tonal control here. Masty, please give us a C major triad to get us started. And since my index finger is getting a wee tired, I will conduct by moving my very long baton along the BluesShape.

EZRA: What words should we use?

JON: Use basic vowel sounds that feel comfortable. For now, follow the baton.

> Readers, if you wish, work with a clock or a watch that has a second hand that can act as a conductor's baton. Below is a simplified BluesShape clock showing the Roman numerals in place of the twelve hour numbers. Or simply go to fig. 5.2, the BluesShape on page 63, and follow the BluesShape at any tempo. Cycle back as often as you like.
>
> Try dancing to the clock's conducting, or let the clock inspire the flow of a theater scene, the telling of a story, or the planning of an evening party meal. Sometimes it's nice to be told when to do something, and your work doesn't have to be in real time; you can really relax with this concept.

Fig. 5.3. Simple BluesShape Clock

JON: Sorry to interrupt you, CreW. Let's do some singing.

CreW sings as a chorus quite beautifully. I join in and find it very uplifting.

JON: Who would like to sing a solo, once through?

Masty volunteers and sings a lovely pass through the BluesShape.

MASTY: I find it easy. I simply shape the basic sound dimensions—dynamics, rhythm, direction, and articulation—to the intensities of the progression.

JON: Like we do in our everyday use of language. CreW, I would like each of you to try using your voices to the BluesShape during the week.

CHESTER: I feel uncomfortable singing by myself.

JON: That's understandable, Chester, but there is a benefit to singing. As I have mentioned, singing is uplifting for me—it increases my sense of well-being. Singing makes your body an instrument and, in my opinion, there is no better way to *touch* music, to feel its power, than through singing, and dancing.

Let's grab our instruments for some more playing with BluesShape. Please follow my baton at the whiteboard again. Let's try using just pure rhythmic sounds. Use muted strings, clapping of hands, tapping of pads, valves, etc. Think percussion ensemble on these variations. I may at times move rather quickly through the BluesShape.

I move through the shape a number of times, varying my speed, sometimes taking only a couple of seconds for a pass-through.

MASTY: Wow, that was intense. What were you thinking?

JON: I made the BluesShape the under-all form *and* the over-all form. I moved through twelve times at three different speeds: a I chord speed, a IV chord speed, and a really fast V chord speed; and finally, a thirteenth time at I chord speed for a final cadence. So it's like that chicken or egg conundrum. I just made the egg the chicken, and the chicken the egg. Just like you are exactly the same person you were at birth, but totally different.

ROBERTO: Now I'm really confused!

JON: So am I, but it felt good. Confusion—at least a healthy variety, let's call it curiosity—is a good springboard for creative thinking.

BluesShape can be made to last for any amount of time. At home, try clapping, singing, playing, speaking, dancing, and breathing BluesShape variations. Let your imaginations explore this simple but rich form. To conclude, here is a poem I composed using BlueShape titled "The Walker." The poem is fairly intense. Above each line I have placed the BluesShape Roman numeral so you can follow the intensity level of each line.

"THE WALKER": A BLUESSHAPE-INSPIRED POEM

The Walker

I

The smoothness of the frozen pond was like fine glass

IV

except for a distant shape breaking the line of smoothness

I

the steady wind further polished the pond's surface

I

and the evening sun burnished the surface to an even tan

IV

except for that distant shape a bit closer now to a distant walker

IV

to whom the object became clearer but still unknown, a creature, a limb,
a forgotten article?

I

the surface slid smoothly beneath the walker's soles, silently

I

she moved effortlessly closer to the seemingly benign object

V

that suddenly grew with a horrid cracking sound and tear that ripped the ice

IV

and raced towards the walker pulling her quickly into the pond screaming

I

then silence as she disappeared below the pond's now scarred surface

V

in horror I raced towards the walker numbly imagining a plan of rescue

I

and silently offering a prayer

So, CreW, try your hand at working with BluesShape. Let's see what ideas get stirred up for our next meeting. Right now let's talk about a CreW field trip.

A CreW Museum Field Trip

JON: Start to observe the forms all around us, and in us. The life of each person is an incredible form that develops every day. Observe our fellow artists, dancers, writers, photographers, painters, and sculptors, and how they develop their compositional forms. It's time for a field trip to a veritable warehouse of forms.

EZRA: Where to, Jon? Home Depot?

JON: No, Ezra, the Museum of Fine Arts, Boston. I would like each of you to spend some time during the week observing forms at the MFA, or a museum of your choice. Let the visual forms inspire some sound forms and ideas.

BRUNO: Should we work from our favorite artists as we did with our favorite composer theme?

JON: If you wish. Try to let the ideas during your museum visit come to you. Effortlessly. Let over-all form and BluesShape explorations inspire you. You have a double assignment: museum inspirations and BluesShape inspirations. Any questions?

> Visual artists, instead of a museum visit, how about attending a concert from which to draw inspiration? Of course, a museum visit is fine also. I like to check out polar opposites for inspiration. Wearing a hat you would never have worn before. What? Check out an opera. Mud wrestling?!

THE "BEBOP SPEEDWAY" FINALE

BRUNO: Jon, you mentioned that we would try my "Bebop Speedway" Charlie Parker–inspired piece this week.

JON: Let's go for it, Bruno. I hope everyone worked on the Charlie Parker blues heads you grabbed last week for Bruno's "Bebop Speedway."

BRUNO: I thought of an over-all form, also. I guess it's a story of sorts.

JON: Let's hear it.

BRUNO: We first need to choose a winner of the race. I thought we could toss a coin, or draw straws?

JON: So, there is an aleatoric, or chance, operation to your piece also, Bruno.

BRUNO: If you say so, Jon.

Bruno takes seven small pieces of paper, one with a smiley face, and places them in a hat for a drawing to choose a winner. Yuto picks the winning smiley face.

JON: So what does Yuto, the soon-to-be winner, get?

BRUNO: A chance to play two "victory" laps: two solo choruses improvising on his chosen blues. So let's begin with Jon saying "Start your engines," at which point we all make engine-like rumbling sounds. Then Jon gives a brisk count off and we begin our bebop blues melodies, all together. After a while, Jon points at one of the "losers," and that player should make their melody begin to "crash" or fall apart and move to silence. Everyone else keep going, crash by crash, until only Yuto will be left playing his blues head. The losers should gradually begin to provide accompaniment for Yuto's victory solo and final statement of his head. Yuto, what is your blues tune?

YUTO: "Air Conditioning," a B-flat Charlie Parker blues.

BRUNO: Okay, soon-to-be losers, play some B-flat blues changes behind Yuto, the soon-to-be winner, for his two victory solo choruses. Jon, let's try this from the top.

JON: Start your engines!

CreW heartily responds with convincing enginelike sounds. I give a brisk count-off and CreW races off with their bebop themes. I gradually cue the losers, one by one, who musically roll over and crash their melodies. Then they support the "Bebop Speedway" winner Yuto and his final victory solo laps.

JON: Congratulations, Yuto! What a fitting way to finish week five, our explorations with seeing, hearing, and playing with form. Have a wonderful field trip to the museum, and enjoy your BluesShape explorations.

> I hope that wasn't too technical for you. Chords are fun to work with. I'm fascinated with them, and I've even written a book, *The Chord Factory*, that really gets surgically into chords.
>
> The BluesShape concept is one of many form possibilities that can act as a catalyst to spark and guide our creative ideas. The uniqueness of BluesShape is that sections are indicated as well as levels of intensity. Remember to let BluesShape last as long or as briefly as you wish—an hour, a few seconds—cycling through as often as you wish.
>
> BluesShape is a nice way to see how looking at a tradition—in this case, a traditional blues—from another angle can open us up to some really new possibilities. Speaking of working from a traditional form as catalyst for new ideas, the English sculptor Henry Moore chose the human body, a pretty traditional form, I'd say, for his decidedly nontraditional work.
>
> I am really excited to see, and hear, how my fellow artists use BluesShape to inspire their particular medium.

CHAPTER 6 – WEEK 6
FORM 201: THE BLUESSHAPE AND MUSEUM FIELD TRIP PIECES

You can't use up creativity. The more you use, the more you have.

—Maya Angelou

THE BLUESSHAPE PIECES

JON: Greetings, CreW. Bruno is sick today so we have a special guest, Az. Welcome, Az, and thank you for being a part of the workshop this morning.

AZ: Good morning, everyone.

JON: CreW, I hope you drew some inspiration from our over-all form discussion last week. We covered a spectrum of form possibilities from the "letter" forms like AABA and ABRA-CADABRA to BluesShape, a form concept adapted from a tried and true traditional form, a 12-bar blues progression.

TIM: Last week you mentioned using BluesShape form with anything in the universe. For my first try I used BluesShape to inspire two simple melodies.

JON: I look forward to hearing your melodies, Tim, and since you are a music artist, using BluesShape to inspire melodies makes perfect sense. Please continue.

TIM: The first melody is pretty simple, applying one note to each level of intensity of the BluesShape. In the second example I tried to achieve each intensity level with several notes.

JON: Can you pass them out?

Working in a new art medium, visual or aural, for the first time can be exciting, and may inspire a fresh approach to our primary medium. The new experience is perfect since we have not yet developed any shoulds or coulds in that new medium. So even nonmusicians, try and play Tim's "BluesShape Melodies." Find a piano, and a helpful friend, if needed. I have sketched in the note names below the notes of the lines to help you. Moving slowly is fine. Can you hear the points of rest and nonrest?

TIM'S "TWO BLUESSHAPE MELODIES"

Fig. 6.1. Tim's "Two BluesShape Melodies"

TIM: Is this what you wanted for a BluesShape piece?

JON: These are perfect examples of using BluesShape form. I'm happy that you were inspired to use traditional notation to express a BluesShape idea.

MASTY'S "BLUESSHAPE PROGRESSION"

MASTY: How about using good old chord symbols with BluesShape?

JON: A great idea, Masty.

MASTY: I have been learning about these really cool slash chords in harmony, and realized that they each have different levels of intensity. I have sketched out a progression using chord symbols and traditional notation. I am enjoying the BluesShape concept, and I like the way it gives me a refreshing technique with which to build harmonic progressions.

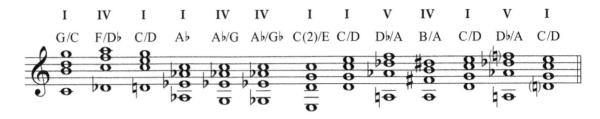

Fig. 6.2. Masty's "BluesShape Progression"

Masty passes out her BluesShape idea, plays her progression, and really captures the concept with her array of slash chords.

JON: That's a wonderful example, Masty, and really works well.

EZRA: I apologize if I digress and if this comment is too obvious. It seems that the function of the ideas we have been discussing is to create communication *through* a composition, and creating its over-all form.

JON: A very astute observation and connection to our activities in CreW, Ezra. We began the semester with developing communication within ourselves and with others. We looked at and used various notation media and other compositional building blocks to communicate our compositional and improvisational ideas to others. Now we are observing the underlying communication systems within compositions. Later in today's class, we will observe these communication systems at work with our inspirations from our museum visits.

> Nonmusicians, I hope you found a friend to help you hear Tim's simple melodies. Remember that the progression of intensities of BluesShape works in all media. In fact, our guest today, Az, is about to get us dancing with some virtual skydiving!

AZ'S "SKYDIVING BLUES"

AZ: Jon, may I share a BluesShape idea I have?

JON: Of course.

AZ: Bruno mentioned that you were working with BluesShape this week. I became familiar with this concept while reading about BluesShape in the form chapter of your book *The Guitarist's Guide to Composing and Improvising*. So I have an idea. I hope it's not too far out. It came to me pretty naturally. I have gone skydiving a few times, and realized that there is a relationship between the sport of skydiving and BluesShape. They both exhibit an interesting progression of intensity levels.

JON: Go for it, Az.

AZ: I call this piece "Skydiving Blues." Here is a sheet I created last night. This piece does not exactly follow BluesShape but it does work with the three levels of I, IV, and V chord intensities. I would like the workshop to try first dancing to the scenario. I feel that getting our bodies involved first will inspire our playing.

JON: Laudable work, Az.

AZ: Jon, I will need your help as conductor here.

JON: My pleasure. I'll conduct by reading your scenario.

AZ: That sounds fine. For now, everyone make your hand the body of the skydiver as you follow along.

> Everyone, including readers, please stand and take your hand and make it represent your body skydiving as we follow Az's "Skydiving Blues." Start with your

hand held high above your head. As your hand (your body) slowly descends past your nose, look down at your hand as it continues its descent toward the floor. I jokingly tell Creative Workshop participants to remember to bring head protection and a flotation device to workshop sessions. Perhaps I wasn't kidding?!

Skydiving Blues

Imagine you are a skydiver, and you are going to parachute from an airplane.
There are several stages that are cued by the conductor.

Cue #1
Introduction: The I Chord
Use your hand here, improvising the feelings before skydiving. This section is the I chord.
It's kind of a nervous I chord. Resting but filled with energy.
You may be . . .
FULL OF ADRENALINE

OVERWHELMED ...... worried

HYPEREXCITED
Build up intensity *gradually* as you prepare for the next cue,
the jump that is the IV chord level.

Cue #2
The Jump: Moving to the IV Chord
Jump, and feel the air rush into your whole body (your hand) as you watch the sky,
the land, grass, streams, rivers, hills; remember, this section is the IV chord.
After a while, as you relax, move your hand's intensity to the I chord level, really enjoying
the scenery for now.

Cue #3
The Opening of the Parachute: The V Chord Moving to the IV Chord
The shock of the parachute opening is the V chord!
You will bounce back up to the sky as the parachute slows you down during
the descent, taking you to a nice, relaxed floating I chord.
Enjoy the trip down as you sail to the ground.

Cue #4
The Landing: This could be a I Chord.
Make up your own landing. This is the "last two bars," and you can either
land gracefully or fall flat because it is your first time.
I hope you enjoyed your journey.

JON: From simple melodies to skydiving, what a leap of medium to try BluesShape with.

AZ: Thanks, Jon, it was fun to sketch it out and to dance to.

How would the progression of intensities that our bodies (our hands) just experienced during our "armchair" skydiving experience affect the contours of a line in a sketch? As an art student, I am fascinated at the depth and power the pressure and release of a pencil point creates visually on the drawing pad.

Try using your entire body to enact "Skydiving Blues." A group of dancers doing this as a canon would be fun.

A BLUESSHAPE PIZZA

JON: CreW, here is a wonderful take on BluesShape. This is from Tim Wolf, a CreW ancestor from the Spring semester of 2014. He let his BluesShape imaginings take him into the kitchen. He can take it from here.

TIM WOLF: I was thinking about how different foods have different intensities, like spiciness and robust flavors, and I wanted to find a way to put a couple of different foods together to form a blues progression. The only way I could think of having all these different intensities together, but having them each distinguished per bite, was through eating a slice of pizza. Eating a pizza slice is like moving through a progression. I just separated the different areas of the slice with different foods, leaving plain cheese pizza for the I chords, stronger flavors for the IV chords, and real spicy foods for the V chords. The final resolution became a ring of hot sauce right before the crust—a final V-I, which I thought was cool.

JON: Cool? That was brilliant, and it was delicious, too!

As you can see, anything in the universe, including pizza-making, is workable as a medium with BluesShape. BluesShape is a simple study form for us right now, but a powerful one because of that magic formula of repetition and contrast and return, and a satisfying, balanced flow of intensity levels with a built-in high point, that V chord.

I must thank Tim Wolf again for his pizza, and the rest of the Spring 2014 Creative Workshop Ensemble for bringing to life an operetta I composed for my granddaughter, Isabel Rose. The instrumentation is voice, slide whistle, mandolin, guitar, bass, and percussion. For the characters we had several finger puppets including Louis Armstrong, Marilyn Monroe, Puccini, Miss Piggy, and, of course, me.

The entire workshop responded with a hearty "CUTE!!!!!"

Fig. 6.3. Tim Wolf's "BluesShape Pizza"

I must mention the finger puppets again. The workshop loved using puppets, and I discovered that they became wonderful creative vehicles for the students along with their instruments. They helped some of the students overcome creative shyness. Consider finger puppets for your creative teaching and performance endeavors. The Unemployed Philosophers Guild has a great collection of finger puppets, including Buddha!

MUSEUM FIELD TRIP–INSPIRED PIECES
YUTO'S INSPIRATION: EDVARD MUNCH MEETS BLUESSHAPE

JON: So how did everyone's field trip to the museum go?

YUTO: I was moved by Edvard Munch's *The Scream* at the Museum of Fine Arts. I didn't bring in a music piece but a visual piece that is inspired by BluesShape. I made a cartoon flip book. I drew a series of caricatures of *The Scream* that went through intensity levels following the BluesShape. My caricature of the original is obviously representing the V chord.

This line from Munch's diary inspired the image for him. It is like a verbal thumbnail of the final painting.

> *I was walking along a path with two friends—the sun was setting— suddenly the sky turned blood red—I paused, feeling exhausted, and leaned on the fence—there was blood, and tongues of fire above the blue-black fjord, and the city—my friends walked on, and I stood there trembling with anxiety—and I sensed an infinite scream passing through nature.*
>
> —Edvard Munch

JON: Thank you for the passage, Yuto, and for the flip book. Your artistic skills are evident here.

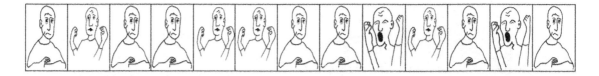

Fig. 6.4. Yuto's Edvard Munch Flip Book

To get a flip book effect, place the left-most panel of fig. 6.4. between your left and right index fingers with your other fingers straightened, nails facing you. Use your thumbs as a "spacer." Close one eye, and then simply slide your hands as a unit to the right exposing the other panels one at a time. Experiment with various speeds.

This is a wonderful example of multimedia conceptualization—a silent, visual BluesShape progression of screams portrayed as a flip book.

"THE BISBEE CHUNK OPUS": JOHN BISBEE, MAKING A POINT

JON: I am always very inspired by trips to museums. In fact, last weekend I was performing with the Portland Symphony Orchestra in Maine, and visited the Portland Museum of Art as part of my museum visit theme. There I discovered the incredible work of a sculptor named John Bisbee. In an earlier discussion we said that the goal in a composition is to make a point as a focus in developing a subject. In John Bisbee's work he *literally* makes his point, using nails as his underlying form or motif. He uses small nails, brads, and every dimension of nail up to twelve-inch nails or spikes, as his building material—his under-all forms. He bends them, hammers them flat, and welds them to create his works. Here are some photos of his work. These photos do not come close to the experience of standing in front of or peering into the works, some of which are quite large. Some weigh a ton! I would like to try and use our CreW team efforts here to see if we can produce some sound art pieces inspired by John Bisbee's sculptures. Here is a wonderful piece titled *CHUNK*.

Fig. 6.5. John Bisbee's *CHUNK* Sculpture

TIM: Those are all nails, Jon?

JON: Yes, they're actually really big nails that, as you can see, produce a perfect, smooth sphere. This piece feels delicate to look at—not unlike the head of seeds on a dandelion just before you blow them away. How do you think we could draw upon this sculpture to build a music piece?

TIM: We must first find our musical nail, the sound motif to build with.

JON: Keep going.

TIM: Let's simply use one pitch to be our basic nail motif. Each time the pitch is played, another "nail" is produced. Let's all begin on a chosen pitch, in unison—say, middle E, for now. We begin with just a few nail notes, occasional attacks of unison E notes. We grow the sphere from its center simply through the introduction of more rhythmic activity of notes, the gradual introduction of E notes an octave higher and lower, and use dynamic growth, getting louder!

JON: That's a great plan, Tim.

MASTY: We should have different sizes of notes, like the nails, creating an augmented triad that grows with the octaves.

JON: Nice idea, Masty. Ezra and Roberto can be E note nailers, you can be a G-sharp nailer, and Az can be a C-natural nailer. The rest of us can be percussionists creating ambience. I think the most important and difficult aspect is to continue to repeat notes once they are introduced to maintain intensity. Each of you will be responsible for the expansion of the sphere. I feel this piece will take some serious energy. I'll conduct. So each of us is, in a sense, building our own sphere, and together we're creating a beautiful sound sphere.

Are you ready? Sounds simple enough? Be patient. When we finally reach full size let's have a lights-out dramatic ending. I'll give a clean cut with my head for our ending.

> When I conduct this workshop interpretation of John Bisbee's *CHUNK*, I am actually dancing with my entire body, hopefully guiding the workshop to musically build John Bisbee's piece from one nail to a fully developed sphere.
>
> You can complete your interpretation in a few seconds; one continuous brush stroke, a simple dance gesture?
>
> I just had another flash of Georges Seurat, a neo-impressionistic pointillist, painting as we play, each touch of his brush tip a nail of Bisbee's *CHUNK*. Seurat believed that a painter could create harmony and emotion in a painting with color as a musician creates harmony and emotion with counterpoint.
>
> How would you interpret the building of *CHUNK* with your medium? At the moment I am actually hearing a wild poem in my imagination, growing bit by bitbit by bitbitbit . . . I'd better stop there for now!

I begin to conduct and the workshop starts to play fairly confidently. Bits of notes, more bits of notes, and as the sound sphere tries to grow through activity and register and volume, I notice that the inner density is being lost, so I begin verbally coaching.

JON: Don't stop playing the original notes! Keep them going!

I stand, suggesting with my hands and arms the present size of our sound sphere. The workshop is tiring, but I encourage them.

JON: Keep going!!

I stand taller, suggesting further growth of our sphere.

JON: Keep going! GO! . . . GO! . . . GO! GOOOOO!!!!!!!!!!!!!

And I finally give a clean cutoff. Some comments percolate from the workshop.

"Wow, that was exhausting!"

"We really nailed that!"

JON: I know. Wonderful playing, and a great example of why the basic sound dimensions are aptly named. The use of register, rhythm, dynamics, and direction really does create a physical structure, in this case a John Bisbee sphere. I'm psyched! Let's try another Bisbee piece.

CHESTER: Can we take a break first?

JON: Sure. Sit back, CreW, and please let me share a fantasy of mine with you. We can try another Bisbee-inspired piece later.

> *So you see, imagination needs moodling—long, inefficient, happy idling, dawdling and puttering.*
> —Brenda Ueland

JON'S DOODLING AND NOODLING FANTASY

JON: Speaking of visual art, I love to doodle.

I go to the whiteboard and sketch two of my doodles.

Fig. 6.6. Jon's First Doodle   Fig. 6.7. Jon's Second Doodle

JON: These doodles share an underlying motif of some sort and are really nonrepresentational; I am not trying to produce anything in particular. And I strongly disagree with the dictionary's version of the word.

doo-dle: verb (intrans.); to scribble absentmindedly: *he was only doodling in the margin.*

I happen to take my doodling very seriously. Only doodling?! I strongly feel that absentmindedness, or daydreaming, is an honorable trait, and in that state some wonderful things can happen—like meditation, or a wonderful doodle.

In fact, I sometimes imagine what one of my doodles would look like executed by the American pop artist Roy Lichtenstein, on a 10 x 12-foot canvas, using black, white, and yellow acrylics for dramatic effect, and hung in the MFA!

CHESTER: Fat chance.

JON: Thanks for the encouraging words, Chester.

CreW, do you think any of the works you viewed during your museum visit started out as doodles? Yes, Yuto?

YUTO: I think that many works of art start out as doodles. In the art world, these doodles are called preliminary sketches, or thumbnail sketches.

JON: And would you consider these doodles, or thumbnail sketches, under-all or over-all form?

YUTO: I would say it is an under-all part of the over-all process of creating the final composition; a microcosmic look at the final work.

JON: Good, Yuto. It is good to know where you are going before you start. Much like writing a murder mystery. The author has to know whodunit, and why, before starting to write that best seller.

Now, CreW, are any of you fellow doodlers?

A chorus of voices:

"I am."

"Me too."

"Yo."

JON: It seems there is a doodling clan amongst us. This wonderfully mindless state of doodling exists in music also, where it's called "noodling." And here is the dictionary's version of this sacred state. They blew this definition also!

noo-dle: verb (intrans.); to improvise or play casually on a musical instrument: *tapes of him noodling on his guitar.*

The dictionary suggests that improvisation is a casual endeavor. I beg to differ! I'm sharing my affection for these two noble pursuits, doodling and noodling, with good reason. These are states that can produce wonderful creative fruit. The composer and conductor Leonard Bernstein said that some of his most productive creative ideas appeared to him in that dreamlike state just before falling asleep, or just before awakening, a state similar to doodling and noodling "consciousness." In fact, it may be fun to get an easel, some drawing paper, pens, and pencils, and along with our instruments, have a doodling/noodling jam.

> Another fantasy of mine is to produce one of those big, beautiful coffee table books, with an accompanying recording, and call it "Doodles and Noodles." I would scavenge the planet in search of wonderful doodles, and record some wonderful noodles.
>
> If you happen to be a proud doodler, as I am, please send me some of your favorites. Pardon if I show my age here, but I remember a wonderful place to collect

doodles was in the old public telephone booth's phone books. The margins of the pages would be covered with all sorts of interesting doodles!

Thanks for letting me share these fantasies of mine with you.

"JON BISBEE'S *STICK, 2002*"

JON: Are you ready to tackle another Bisbee piece?

I hold up a photo of John Bisbee's *Stick, 2002* for the workshop.

Fig. 6.8. Jon Bisbee's *Stick, 2002*.
One ton of welded 12-inch steel spikes.

JON: This is a big, 2000-pound pile, 68 inches tall, of some really big nails. Any suggestions of how we can turn this one-ton sculpture into a piece of music? As you can see, *Stick, 2002* is a powerfully ascending piece of nail sculpture, seeming to rise and disappear into space. Any ideas for how we, as sound sculptors, can achieve this?

ROBERTO: This idea will not last too long but I think it may work. Let's begin by creating an intense foundation of sound, fairly loud, with low register notes, and on cue we begin to ascend pitch-wise and tempo-wise but at the same time getting softer and softer, moving into silence.

JON: Good, Roberto, short and sweet, but intense; let's go for it.

MASTY: Would it help if we added tritones to add to the intensity and texture of the piece?

JON: Good idea.

CHESTER: Hold it! Can you please refresh my memory as to what a tritone is?

JON: A tritone is an interval distance of three whole steps.

CHESTER: I must admit that my knowledge of intervals is limited. I would rather just play music than have to be thinking of intervals.

JON: Well, Chester, there are some benefits to having to think. Being able to describe elements of music, like intervals, for example, is important for the creative musician. An awareness of the sounds and shapes of intervals is a really valuable tool. Remember that what at first needs diligent intellectual study eventually becomes part of your instinct. Our incredible ability with language is testament to this. Remember those words "intellistinctual" and "instinctuallectual"

I used in our first meeting? I keep looking for a word that describes a balance between our intellect and instinct working together. I believe in one whole brain, at work creatively.

CHESTER: Thanks, Jon, I will really try to learn my intervals better.

JON: Great. Your work will really help with our next theme, Intervals of Time and Space.

CHESTER: Sounds sci-fi.

Chester's questioning the need for academic training for an inspired artist like him is nothing new. Attending a major museum exhibition of a particular artist's work, generally hung chronologically, may produce an answer to his query. In fact, a library visit to those oversized coffee table books of an artist's life work may be easier and cheaper than a visit to the museum. I recently thumbed through folios of Joán Miró, Marc Chagall, and Salvador Dalí, and the visual journey was mind-boggling.

Their careers began with representational works and developed into incredibly fresh, abstract images. I strongly feel that any artwork is representational of something; making the connection is the fun part.

I must take Chester aside and suggest a library visit for him.

In the world of jazz, the stories of Mile Davis's Juilliard days and John Coltrane's studies of Nicolas Slonimsky's *Thesaurus of Scales and Melodic Patterns* also show that the study of tradition can provide a wellspring of inspiration.

I believe it was Pablo Picasso who said, "Learn the rules before you break them."

JON: Let's try bringing Bisbee's *Stick, 2002* sculpture to musical life. Following Roberto's idea, let's begin together, intensely creating a solid foundation with low register notes, and tritones if you wish, loudly at first. On my cue, begin to move your notes with my hands, upward and accelerating at the same time but getting softer until silence. Do not slow down! This will only last about forty-three seconds. Let's try it. Ready, on my cue.

CreW brings *Stick, 2002* to life with an exciting, powerful statement.

Tim's "Jackson Pollock–Inspired Opus"

TIM: Jon, I have another short museum piece that only lasts for thirty seconds at most. It's a Jackson Pollock–inspired piece.

JON: Okay, Tim, lead us on.

TIM: There are some nice Jackson Pollock paintings at the MFA, and they stirred memories of the film *Pollock* that I saw a few years ago. When I first looked at a Pollock painting, I only felt confusion, but thanks to the movie and further visits to observe Pollock pieces, I've come to realize the incredible compositional power in them. I don't have one piece in mind. I only have a concept that we can play with. The canvas seems like a drum to Pollock. His painting motions are percussive at times, with the hurlings and slappings of paint on canvas. So each of us will activate a color that will be combined with intensity of attack and register. String players, you will be slapping the fingerboard.

Tim strikes his fingerboard with his palm intensely. SLAP! SLAP!

Horns and percussion get a slapping effect by playing strong, accented attacks.

TIM: I'll only need five colors, and the white of the canvas, of course. I'll conduct the SLAPS of colors with slapping gestures at each player. For the warmer colors slap hard and in low register, for the cooler colors slap hard and in high register. It's that simple. Roberto, you are gray; Ezra, you are medium blue; Yuto, you are red; Chester, you are yellow; Masty, you are purple; and Az, you are white, or the bare canvas, so you slap silence.

AZ: I slap silence? That sounds like a Zen koan.

Tim begins giving cues to the various players with their assigned colors. SLAP! . . . SLAP!! . . . SLAP!!, and about thirty seconds later finishes up.

TIM: Thank you, my fellow workshop members.

JON: Nice piece, Tim.

> Give a listen to the pianist Cecil Taylor, a very inspiring musician whose work, for me, has always stimulated thoughts of Jackson Pollock's work. Out of what at first feels to me like piano keyboard chaos, a brilliant sense of development and composition emerges. The works of both of these artists evoke an incredibly similar dance.

Intervals of Time and Space

TIM: Jon, when does under-all form become over-all form? Your discussion about doodles and noodles got me thinking.

JON: It's up to the artist. I'm sure some artists feel that their "final" painting composition or music composition is never completed even after piles of sketches. As you know, I love each of my doodles and consider each a masterpiece. Probably because I don't take them too seriously, which is food for thought.

Thanks, Tim, for bringing up this question, and thanks, Chester, for asking about the tritone. Our next theme is Under-all forms: Intervals of Time and Space. We will focus microscopically on the beauty of the under-all forms of art: intervals of direction, dynamics, rhythm, and articulation. They are the microcosms of the macrocosm.

CHESTER: What?!

JON: That's just fancy lingo for under- and over-all forms.

Assignment for Week 7

JON: I have a simple assignment for everyone this week. I would like you to hunt for the simplest melodies you can think of. Next week we will build a concerto from some of them. And thank you for letting me share my doodles and noodles with you. CreW techniques work with all idioms and levels of musicianship, and I dream of the day that I can try some CreW concepts and ideas with the Boston Symphony Orchestra. What great therapy it would be for them. The closest I have come so far has been working with the Wellesley Middle School thirty-member Concert Band.

CHESTER: Close, but no cigar.

JON: Jeez, thanks, Chester.

NOTES, DOODLES, AND NOODLES

CHAPTER 7 – WEEK 7
FORM 301: UNDER-ALL FORMS: INTERVALS OF TIME AND SPACE

Everything has its beauty but not everyone sees it. —Chinese proverb

INTERVALS OF TIME AND SPACE

JON: Hello, CreW. As you have probably noticed, in our form explorations we have mainly been working from fairly large forms for inspiration: six foot tall metal sculptures, 8 x 13–foot Jackson Pollock canvases, skydiving expeditions, speedways, and coronations. Now let's take out our virtual microscopes and look at the "cellular" forms, the organisms that make art "tick": the intervals of time and space, the basic sound, visual, and spatial dimensions, the super-under-all forms.

CHESTER: Jon, you mentioned "intervals of time and space" last week also. What's up with that?

JON: "Intervals of time and space" is simply my trying-to-be-cute title for the under-all forms, the intervals of direction(up and down), rhythm (width), dynamics (depth), and articulation (contour) that make up the basic motif building blocks in music and visual art.

SPEAKING OF LANGUAGE

CHESTER: All of those dimensions seem like too much for me to have to think about!

JON: But Chester, you just used all of them.

CHESTER: How? Who? ME?!

JON: Yes, you, and the rest of the workshop, and many people on this planet are masters of an incredible improvisational art, spoken language. All the basic sound dimensions are used in a very exacting manner every time we speak.

MASTY: Cool!

JON: Nice delivery, Masty. In fact, if we weren't looking, we could all tell that was Masty speaking, just by hearing one word, "cool." Why? Bruno?

BRUNO: Because she has a special way of speaking.

JON: Do you mean her personality of speaking?

BRUNO: I guess you can say that.

JON: Masty has decided, instinctually, and after years of practice, what pitch, dynamic level, rhythm, and articulation to use for her delivery of the word "cool," which, as you notice, is much different than each of ours.

> Readers, how does your delivery of the word "cool" sound? How does it compare to Bart Simpson's "cool"?

AN OFTEN-ASKED QUESTION

JON: One of the questions I am asked most often is, "How can I develop my own musical/artistic personality?" To answer, I ask the student who their favorite musician is, their hero at the moment. Bruno, who is your present musical hero?

BRUNO: Sonny Rollins at the moment. I've been listening to *The Bridge,* a great album.

JON: And Ezra?

EZRA: Joshua Bell, a really cool violinist.

JON: And how can you tell you are hearing your hero? Yes, Bruno?

BRUNO: I can tell Sonny Rollins from just one note. His attack, tone, how he changes volume in that one note. Sonny likes to repeat a note quite a bit and really uses rhythm, dynamics, and articulation to shape that note. It never gets boring, just one note.

> As with Sonny Rollins's delivery of his music, the delivery, and articulation of language is an actor's bread and butter—how the actor paints with her emotions, her colors. Painters have many different brush stroke articulations, depending on their style.
>
> As I write this book, I first write manually, on yellow paper, with an erasable, red-ink ballpoint pen, and then transfer the ideas to my computer. One day I tried writing with a traditional fountain pen, with black ink, and was astounded that the attack and feel of the fountain pen strongly controlled my writing ideas, my delivery. I enjoyed the stimulation, and now I keep the fountain pen nearby as a potential catalyst for when my red-ink ballpoint pen hits a creative block.

JON: To answer that often-asked question for yourself, don't just come up with an idea; learn to *deliver* your idea with creative use of the basic sound dimensions, and shape your musical voice just as you shape your speaking voice. Remember that it's not how much you've got that's important, it's how well you use what you've got.

EZRA: So when we play notes, be aware of their tops and bottoms, and sides, fronts, and backs?

JON: That's a great way to think of it, awareness of the dimensions of your idea.

Today let's zoom in microscopically on each of the sound dimensions and the visual and spatial dimensions they create. Today may be our most technically intellectual language session of the semester. And for good reason. We are getting down to details!

THE DYNAMIC DIMENSION: HOW CLOSE? HOW FAR?

JON: We will begin with what I feel is the most important sound dimension, dynamics. Close your eyes for a moment, please. If I speak the word "cool" repeatedly and change how loudly I'm speaking, what does it seem like the word is doing? Give a listen.

cool.... cool.... cool.... cool.... cool.... cool.... cool.... cool.... cool .... cool.... cool.... cool.... cool.... cool.... cool.... cool.... cool....

The workshop reacts:

"It seems like the word is getting larger or smaller."

"It seems like the word is at first coming closer, then as you spoke more softly it moved away."

JON: Good. Dynamics creates depth, or how close or far away a sound is, and a sense of size.

EZRA: Why do you feel that dynamics is the most important dimension, Jon?

JON: Let's use a scenario of a duet for simplicity. If you are accompanying the great Joshua Bell and you are playing too loudly, Joshua's greatness, his delivery, is not so great anymore. All the other sound dimensions are meaningless when the dynamic level doesn't work. In fact, silence is considered the ultimate form.

THE RHYTHMIC DIMENSION: HOW FAST? HOW SLOW?

JON: Next in importance, and now that I think of it, maybe just as important as the dynamic dimension, is the rhythmic dimension. We have a lot of experience and control with rhythm, since we have been using it for quite a while in the rhythm of our talk, our walk, our writing, reading, and eating, knocking on doors. Close your eyes again and give a listen. What is the word "cool" doing now, as I speak it?

cool......................cool...............cool.........cool......cool...cool..cool.cool........cool.

ROBERTO: The word is simply speeding up or slowing down, creating a wide or squinched up feeling of width.

JON: Good observation, Roberto; rhythm creates the dimension of width and a quality of width.

YUTO: Is silence a dimension? I notice that dynamics and rhythm depend on it.

JON: That's a great perception, Yuto. Silence is a powerful dimension against which all the sound dimensions are perceived. In visual art silence is the blank canvas, and when an image, a brush stroke, or positive space is created, the "silent" space around it is called the "negative" space. It is the interplay between the positive and negative spaces that makes or breaks a composition. I'll share a fun art technique with you later that really brings you into that interplay.

THE ARTICULATION (TONE COLOR) DIMENSION: HOW ROUND? HOW SHARP?

JON: Bruno, let's talk about Sonny Rollins again for a moment.

BRUNO: My pleasure, Jon. I enjoy when Sonny repeats a pitch and explores attacking that note in various ways, creating speechlike syllable sounds. Great singers like Ella Fitzgerald, Chet Baker, and Louis Armstrong really create a variety of sharp and smooth colors with their scat syllables!

JON: Good point. Articulation is the manner of musical speech. Here is a scat quote from the great jazz singer Sarah Vaughan. I'll scratch it on the board. Try scat singing next time you're in the shower to discover your favorite syllables. Each of us has our own personal scat singing vocabulary.

Shoo-doo-shoo-bee-ooo-bee   —Sarah Vaughan

Readers, how is your shower scat singing? What scat syllables do you like to use, especially when you forget the lyrics of that tune you are crooning? Exploring the roundness and sharpness of syllables and their interplay in scat singing is very therapeutic.

THE PITCH INTERVAL (DIRECTION) DIMENSION: HOW UP? HOW DOWN?

JON: Before we look at a pitch interval that consists of two notes, I would like to get out our musical microscopes and put a single note on the slide. As we look at and listen closely to that note, we observe an incredible form at play, the note's overtone series, also called its "harmonic series." These are musical tones that may be heard along with the original note.

Here is a note C and its first sixteen overtones. The darkened notes are fairly "out of tune" relative to our everyday western European equal tempered system.

THE OVERTONE SERIES

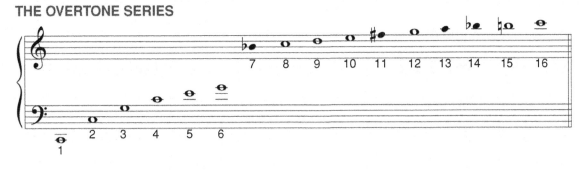

Fig. 7.1. The Overtone Series

Overtones are what "paint" an instrument's tone color or "timbre." Each instrument has its particular overtone series, which is generated by its physical parameters. Is it a string instrument? Is it made of wood or brass? Is it of a cylindrical or conical shape? These conditions affect an instrument's harmonics and determine that instrument's tone color. A favorite book of mine on this subject is *Horns, Strings, and Harmony,* by Arthur Benade.

JON: It takes two notes to create an interval. When played together, each note's overtones meet and either "get along," creating consonance, or "don't get along," creating dissonance.

TIM: So each interval has its own color personality. Some are mild-tempered, and some have an attitude.

JON: An apt description, Tim.

TIM: *Twentieth Century Harmony* by Vincent Persichetti is a book that gets into detail about pitch intervals as well as many other facets of contemporary harmony.

JON: That is a great book, Tim, thanks for the suggestion. Here's a cool quote from the book.

> *Intervals can follow each other in any order, and may be arranged to form any pattern of tension interplay.*   —Vincent Persichetti

SIMPLE MELODIES

JON: I asked all of you to find some simple melodies to get us started today with our explorations of the under-all forms.

TIM: Jon, I have a simple song that I believe is the world's most well-known and often-sung melody, "Happy Birthday." All the international students that I asked were aware of it, and have actually sung it at one time or another.

JON: Well, one thing everyone worldwide has in common is having a birthday, so perhaps you're right.

Let me write "Happy Birthday" on the board. And while I'm at the board, what other simple melodies should I note?

CreW comes up with the following list:

Happy Birthday   Mary Had a Little Lamb
Old MacDonald   Danny Boy
Frère Jacques   Row Row Row Your Boat
Greensleeves   Jingle Bells
Amazing Grace

JON: That's a good start. They will come in handy for our under-all form explorations.

LET'S ANSWER THAT OFTEN-ASKED QUESTION

JON: Let's take another look at that often-asked question, "How can I create my own musical–artistic personality?" We will explore delivering a musical idea with creative use of the basic sound dimensions to shape your musical voice just as you shape your speaking voice.

Let's begin with the "Happy Birthday" theme. Can anyone play it?

CHESTER: It's such a simple song, who couldn't play it?

JON: Okay, Chester, go right ahead.

CHESTER: Any key?

JON: Any key is fine.

Chester proceeds, and has a tough and embarrassing time finding the right notes.

CHESTER: Jeez, I didn't think it would be that hard.

JON: The only reason that I can play the "Happy Birthday" theme on my instrument right now is because I did a lot of *intellectual* homework on hearing and seeing pitch intervals, inside my head and on my instrument. Being able to do this is essential for the improviser.

TIM: How can we start to be able to do that?

JON: Later I will share a simple ear study with you. Right now, everyone please start on the note G and work out "Happy Birthday" for a moment until you have it somewhat under your fingers. That larger interval in the melody is an octave, by the way. Let me know when you have the melody worked out, and then we will put it through some variations.

After a few moments, the workshop perks up:

"Got it."

"I'm cool."

"I'm fine with it, that octave clue helped out nicely."

The workshop reaches a consensus on "Happy Birthday."

> Fellow visual artists, without peeking, can you sketch, from memory, the face of a very simple, common cartoon character you have been looking at for years? How about Minnie Mouse, Charlie Brown, Tintin? Go ahead and try, then compare your drawing to the actual cartoon character. Is it as challenging for you to capture that cartoon image as it is for Chester to play "Happy Birthday" from memory? After that peek at the actual cartoon character, try a "by memory" sketch

again. It's amazing how those simple strokes you've been looking at for years can be so elusive to both mind and hand.

THE "HAPPY BIRTHDAY" THEME GOES EXPLORING

JON: Now that we have "Happy Birthday" under our fingers, let's breathe some musical life into it and work on our deliveries.

CHESTER: How can we make "Happy Birthday" musical? It's a pretty boring melody.

JON: Well, I happen to think it's a wonderful melody. Our delivery of a musical idea is what makes or breaks that idea. Not unlike telling a joke; if our delivery of a joke is weak, the joke is not very funny, is it? Let's see how musical we can make "Happy Birthday." Just for fun, let's see and hear how many variations of deliveries we can muster. Don't change any notes. Work with the dynamic, rhythm, and articulation sound dimensions to shape your variation. First I'll put the chord progression for "Happy Birthday" on the board."

| C | G7 | D-7 G7 | C | G-7 C7 | F | C G7 | C |

JON: Yuto, please provide accompaniment for our "Happy Birthday" variations today. Traditionally "Happy Birthday" is a waltz. For our variations we can make it any meter and groove we wish.

BRUNO: I'd like to do it in 4/4 swing.

JON: Okay, Bruno and Yuto, swing it, cats.

EZRA: I like how they played, but there was no improvisation. They kept playing the melody over and over.

JON: There's actually plenty of improvisation happening—improvisation with the sound dimensions.

MASTY: Jon, here is a classical version. Yuto, let's do it as a waltz.

Masty and Yuto play a lovely classical rendition of "Happy Birthday."

JON: Ezra, how is Masty and Yuto's version of "Happy Birthday" different from Bruno and Yuto's?

EZRA: It's more gentle, softer, more simple rhythms are used. I like that version also, and now I see that "Happy Birthday" can really be a nice melody.

The workshop continues producing a variety of improvised deliveries of "Happy Birthday," including calypso, bluesy, rock, and funk interpretations.

Now imagine sketching Minnie Mouse's portrait through a series of emotions, something like the workshop members' delivery of "Happy Birthday" in a number of different styles. How about giving Minnie a classical look, perhaps with a Mona Lisa smile?

JON: Now we will put the pitch intervals to work and create some of our own melodic improvisations, and continue to use our imaginations with the other sound dimensions. I realize that you all enjoy improvising melodic solos on jazz, blues, and standard tunes. Where do your improvised melodies come from?

Workshop feedback ensues:

"I use arpeggios from the chord progression."

"I use ideas from transcriptions of solos that I have done."

"I work from the chord shapes to find solo ideas."

JON: All great ideas. Do you remember the Beethoven dream I shared with you?

TIM: I do. Beethoven was getting down on you for not using the original theme as creative melodic material in your improvisation.

JON: Thank you, Tim. The melodic improvisation ideas you guys came up with are great ideas. I love using them also. I have also really tried to take Ludwig's suggestion, and have learned to use a tune's melodic material as much as the tune's chord progression for my melodic improvisations. Let's look at the "Happy Birthday" melody purely for its pitch interval and direction architecture. I would like each of you to find something you feel is "special" in the melody line. Roberto?

ROBERTO: I can see a duet built into the melody. In the first four bars, the first part is the G note repeating while the second part gradually goes up until it reaches the octave G note at the beginning of the second line, then both parts come together. I'm used to working with compound lines, a melody that has two or more inner melodies.

JON: Good observation. Ezra?

EZRA: It looks and sounds like a spring tightening at first and then releasing at the second line like a jack-in-the-box!

JON: Wow, Ezra, you sound as excited as I am about exploring melodies like this. And Bruno?

BRUNO: I think it's cool how the melody clearly states the harmonic accompaniment with no chords.

JON: Another astute observation. When you begin to look at melodies as pure sculpture, having dimensions, you will begin to see a deeper innate beauty in your own melodic improvisations. You can develop from these pure melodic observations.

YUTO: What do you mean by "pure melodic"?

JON: By that I mean finding creative resource in a tune's melody, much like Beethoven taught me in my dream.

> Lets talk cartoons again. Just as the workshop was exploring the under-all melodic details of "Happy Birthday" I thought of the idiosyncratic strokes in a cartoon character's drawing, and how exacting those simple strokes must be. If Mickey's ears and smile or the lovely shape of Charlie Brown's head are not just right, they would be quite different characters.

JON: Let's take a look at these other simple melodies you brought in and find some special things about them.

YUTO: Jon, as I look at these simple melodies, they are not so simple anymore. They have some really nice qualities about them. They are simply beautiful. It's incredible the beauty that is all around us if we just listen and look. There must be a reason why these melodies have been around for so long!

JON: Nicely said, Yuto.

> Yuto's comment is wonderfully like the Chinese proverb that opens this chapter. "Everything has its beauty but not everyone sees it." I am always amazed at the beauty in children's artistic efforts—as much as by seeing a master's work during a visit to a museum.

CHESTER: I'm beginning to like this analytical stuff, as it turns on some lights to help us see and hear things that we may have missed otherwise.

JON: Nicely put, Chester.

JON'S MELODY DIARY

JON: The term "head" in jazz parlance is slang for a tune's melody. When I find a melodic tidbit I like from a tune, I sketch it down and give it a brief pitch interval analysis.

A hand shoots up. "Isn't that piracy?"

JON: No. The segments are not more than four notes in length, and I use them in ways that the composer would not recognize. This analysis helps me use the motif in my improvisations and inspires new compositions.

OTHER SOUND AND SPACE DIMENSION EXPLORATIONS
"CITYSCAPES"

JON: Let's look at some other dimensions. Another of my favorite explorations, rich in the sound dimensions, is a piece I call "CityScapes," in which the city is the actual performer. Find a safe spot, close your eyes, cup your ears with your palms to increase your hearing capability, and simply listen. Listen to the layers of close sounds, medium distant sounds, far away sounds, sounds moving toward you and away, a single unrelenting sound. Of course, you can do this in the country too, but the city, ooh la la! what a rich sound tapestry. In fact, here is a question to get us primed for our next theme, Forms from Mother Nature. Does "CityScapes" work for that theme?

My query engenders some workshop responses:

"Of course not. Sirens don't sound very natural to me!"

"Trucks are loud, and they stink, literally!"

"But everything comes from Mother Nature."

JON: Hold it, CreW. Let's save this debate for later!

Here is another nice piece that explores the dimension of rhythm and taps into a real city phenomenon, rush hour.

"RUSH HOUR RHYTHMS"

JON: I would like everyone to please put your instruments down for a moment and gather by the window. Here are some "snappers" for you to use for this piece. From our fifth-floor vantage point, through these three windows, we can see down to a nice chunk of Boston's Boylston Street. I would like each of you to spot a morning walking commuter as they appear from the left or right. Find your very own commuter now! When you spot your commuter, begin snapping your snapper *exactly* with their footsteps, and continue until your commuter has vanished from the scene. The piece ends with total silence. Is everyone's snapper ready? Okay . . . Go!

Snap! Snap! Snap! Snap! Snap! Snap! Snap! Snap! Snap! Snap! Snap! Snap!

Snap! Snap! Snap! Snap! Snap! Snap! Snap! Snap!

Snap! Snap! Snap! Snap! Snap! Snap! Snap! Snap! Snap! Snap! Snap! Snap! Snap Snap

Snap! Snap! Snap! Snap! Snap! Snap! Snap!

Snap! Snap! Snap! Snap! Snap! Snap! Snap! Snap! Snap! Snap! Snap! Snap! Snap Snap

Snap! Snap! Snap! Snap! Snap! Snap! Snap! Snap! Snap!

Snap! Snap! Snap! Snap! Snap! Snap! Snap! Snap! Snap! Snap! Snap! Snap! Snap Snap

"Rush Hour Rhythms" gradually comes to a conclusion.

EZRA: That would be fun to do with a variety of percussion instruments instead of these snappers.

JON: A great idea. That's exactly what I want you CreWsters to do with workshop-inspired ideas: use them in any ensemble situation to freshen things up.

ROBERTO: This piece reminds me of a chorus of crickets.

JON: Interesting thought, Roberto. Remember that analogy for our Forms from Mother Nature session.

> I would love to try "Rush Hour Rhythms" as a collaborative work with a number of painters, working on one canvas, each painter responding to their commuter's walking rhythm and personality, interpreting that rhythm horizontally and colorfully across the canvas. How about right in Times Square! If the mural comes out yucky, we can always blame the commuters.

WHITE SPACE: "IN SEARCH OF SILENCE"

JON: In this silence study, we will use our voices as instruments and tap into the rich music of spoken language. Here are a poem I've written called "In Search of Silence" and some black felt markers. As you can see, the text is white against the black background. On my cue, I would like all of you to begin reading the poem. Read at a comfortable pace, and maintain that reading pace through the poem. On your second pass through the poem, begin to leave out a word here and there, and blacken out the word with the marker as you do. Continue reading and blackening out words until you eventually attain total silence. Be patient. Leave silent space for the blackened words as you pass them again in your reading. Passing through the poem several times may be needed until total silence is achieved.

Ready . . . Go.

In Search of Silence

Snow is comforting, masking the clutter of cars,
and street corners, the edge of schedules.
Like the beginnings of a meditation, trying to white out
thoughts with each falling repetition of mantra.
The comfort from the glance at snowflakes continuing
their descent against the street lamp is familiar.
And the underlying hope that it never stops, is there.
The snow-white womb feels good during the walks
through the fresh white powder, dustings from the
windblown trees adding a gauze to the landscape.
Leading to almost silence at trail's end.
A squawk of crow, a breath, a pulsing from somewhere?
Not quite the anechoic chamber from
John Cage's search for silence.
In the chamber he experienced two sounds,
his nervous and circulatory systems.
Out here, the invisible drone of plane in the cloud is
inescapable. Yet etchings of silence are there.
As the snow masks the eye and ear
in its blanket of seeming perfection.

JON: Thank you for your reading, and for your patience blackening out all those words. I like the canonic echoes of the words through the piece, and the effect of the voices slowly vanishing into the silence.

Readers, try "In Search of Silence" as a solo piece, and record it. Keep your own pace of reading and blackening the words to silence. It's fun to hear how silence slowly takes over the poem, which is the subject matter!

RHYTHM VOCABULARY STUDY

BRUNO: Jon, since we were working on rhythms earlier, in my jazz improvisation I feel that my rhythmic vocabulary is very limited.

JON: All right, Bruno, here's a fresh copy of "In Search of Silence." Please read the first line.

BRUNO: *Snow is comforting, masking the clutter of cars . . .*

JON: Okay, good. Now play the words with your instrument. Use any pitches you wish but play the *same* rhythms you used when you read it orally.

He tries it.

BRUNO: That's hard.

JON: Do the rhythms again, but now with just one note.

Bruno tries again.

BRUNO: That's cool. I'm playing new rhythms.

JON: Right, and remember that we are masters of language. Why not tap into this power? Now do the whole poem, and try more notes.

BRUNO: Wow, I dig it!

> The jazz cats and hip-hop generation are way into the music of language. The hip-hop artist Tajai says, "Sometimes my rhythms come from scatting. I usually make a scat kind of skeleton and then fill in the words." The book *A Jazz Lexicon* by Robert Gold is testament to the jazz cats' love of rhythm in language, and is a creative source for todays hip-hop artists.

JON: CreW, if you would like to explore articulation and tone color more deeply with your instruments, try playing each individual letter of the alphabet using one note with your instrument, interpreting the various round and sharp sounds of each letter.

CHESTER: How about using Morse code, a rhythmic alphabet for a rhythm piece?

JON: That's a brilliant idea, Chester.

SCRATCHBOARD AND SNOW CRYSTALS

JON: I mentioned earlier that I would show you an art technique that really focuses on positive and negative space. Would you like to try doing some scratchboard?

BRUNO: What is scratchboard, some kind of lottery game?

JON: Scratchboard is a visual art technique in which a sheet of paper or piece of white plastic or ceramic with a highly polished surface is coated with black ink and left to dry. A fine needle-tipped instrument is used to etch away the dried ink, exposing the white undersurface. It's an interesting technique.

TIM: I would like to try.

YUTO: I would, too.

JON: Okay, here's a sheet of scratchboard for each of you.

You may remember earlier this morning I mentioned positive and negative space with regard to a visual art composition.

ROBERTO: Yes, you said that when a shape is created, both a positive and a negative shape are created, and seeing these at the same time is critical in weighing a composition's balance.

JON: Thank you, Roberto.

YUTO: Jon, can you please explain further?

JON: Sure, Yuto.

Everyone, including you readers, hold up one of your hands with fingers spread in front of your eyes. The positive space of the image of your hand is your hand itself, and the negative space is everything else. Try spreading your fingers—the positive space—bending them, stretching them, and notice how the negative space is directly affected.

MASTY: That's pretty cool. I'm in control of the entire universe!

JON: I wouldn't go quite that far, Masty.

I remember in art school our teacher had us work with scratchboard technique to help us observe negative space more clearly. When we make a gesture with a pencil or a brush on white paper we create a positive image. With scratchboard, we will shape an image, but our scratching into the black ink with the etching tool will create the negative space.

MASTY: What should we draw?

JON: I thought we could create some snow crystals, a.k.a. snowflakes.

MASTY: But snowflakes are white, so we are creating the positive image when we scratch.

JON: That's a good point. Well, I would like to produce *black* snowflakes.

BRUNO: Cool. Can I have a sheet of scratchboard also?

JON: Sure. I brought in a snowflake book and some photocopied pages. Please pass these along. Everyone choose one and go to work.

EZRA: It's going to be hard to do it exactly.

JON: A variation is fine. Think of the photo as a basic form to work from, similar to how we worked from the simple melodies this morning. If the snowflake motif is too difficult, imagine your own snowflake. Working from another image would also be fine. Even producing a letter from the alphabet, a black letter, will focus the negative space for you. Keep working on those scratchboards during the week, and we'll have an art show.

TIM: Jon, can you go over that interval ear study you said you would give me?

JON: Sure, Tim.

A Simple Melodic Ear–Hand Study

JON: First choose a simple melody, say "Old MacDonald" for now. Start on any note on your instrument and play "Old MacDonald." Work at it until you learn it, taking intellectual note of the "trickier" intervals. Then, on a wind or brass instrument, start "Old MacDonald" on a note a half step higher than before and work out the melody from this note. On a string instrument, start on the same note but with a different finger, and work it out. Hopefully those intellectual interval observations will help. Continue until you move through all possible starting notes or starting fingers. This study is a simple but powerful tool for learning how to find a melodic line on your instruments.

Next Week's Assignment: Forms from Mother Nature

JON: That was a fun morning. For next week, conjure up some pieces inspired by Mother Nature: weather, waves, wind, trees, bees. Let an aspect of nature show you a piece. Look around, listen around, and smell around. The ideas will come to you. Have a great week, and thanks again for a great session, my fellow CreWsters. And don't forget those scratchboards.

Jon's Scratchboard Snowflake

Dear readers, that includes you, too. Send me one. Here is one of mine. A perfect original, by the way, since no two snowflakes are alike!

Fig. 7.2. Jon's Scratchboard Snowflake

CHAPTER 8 – WEEK 8
FORMS FROM MOTHER NATURE

> *To live a creative life, we must lose our fear of being wrong.*
>
> —Joseph Chilton Pearce

FORMS FROM MOTHER NATURE
THE MORMON TABERNACLE CHOIR OF THE AVIAN WORLD

MASTY: Good, morning, Jon.

JON: Hi, Masty.

MASTY: Jon, you mentioned in the first week of class that you enjoyed bird watching. Have you heard of a South American bird, the Plain-tailed Wren? These birds perform in choirs and are considered the Mormon Tabernacle Choir of the avian world.

JON: This sounds like a perfect fit for today's theme, forms from Mother Nature. CreW, Masty has some bird news for us.

MASTY: I was telling Jon about a bird, the Plain-tailed Wren, that some scientists believe has the most complex song in the animal world. They sing in groups of up to seven birds. Their songs follow an ABCD form; the males sing the A and C sections, the females the B and D sections.

TIM: Hold it! These are birds?

MASTY: Yes, Tim.

JON: Thanks, Masty, for launching our theme for today's session, in which we will explore and draw inspiration from the natural world. And aren't we perfect candidates to be explorers, since we are a part of the natural world? Birds are a natural link for us because of their captivating aural and visual beauty. Bird images are ubiquitous, found in architecture, in paintings of the great masters, in King Tut's tomb paintings, and even on one-dollar bills.

Yes, Bruno?

BRUNO: Certain musicians come to mind. The composer Olivier Messiaen transcribed the songs of birds and used them in his compositions. Saxophonist Roland Kirk would visit a zoo and play duets with the birds and other animals. And how about tunes such as "Blackbird" by the Beatles, and Charlie Parker's "Ornithology"?

> Birds are not only sources for inspiration. They themselves are inspired musicians, dancers, and sculptors. The breeding ritual of the Grey-crowned Crane from Africa includes an elaborate dance that local natives use as a basis for their

own ceremonial dances. Bowerbirds, indigenous birds of Australia, are incredible sculptors and construct intricate bowers and actual huts up to ten feet tall to attract a mate. The bowers are adorned with various shiny objects like glass and coins. One Spotted Bowerbird is reported to have used up to five pounds of roofing nails, stolen from a barn a mile away, to create an elaborate entrance to a bower it had built.

So that's where John Bisbee got his inspiration!

TIM'S "AMOEBA FORM"

TIM: I have a piece that's not inspired by a sound of nature, but by a creature's basic behaviors.

JON: That's a nice use of conceptual art technique, Tim—drawing on natural behavior to inspire one's artwork. Please continue.

TIM: I always enjoyed science in high school, and still have a microscope that I use. I remember in biology studying one-celled creatures like paramecium and amoebas that live in pond water. My piece is called "Amoeba Form." These parts will explain my concepts clearly. The coolest aspect of amoebic life is their reproductive cycle. They simply divide themselves. If we humans did this, it would save so much time in courtship!

JON: And money too—no need for flowers, showers, phone bills, and wedding plan decisions. I digress. Pass out those parts, Tim.

TIM: I'm also suggesting slow chromatic motion to capture the amoebas' subtle ballet.

Amoeba Form
First Movement
On cue, play a note beginning softly.
Depending on your instrument, play this note with a vibrato, or as a tremolo. This is how the amoeba breathes.

Your amoeba (note) can only move chromatically and slowly, since amoebas are very small. Move your amoeba in any direction you wish, but not too quickly, and again, in half steps only. Dynamic variations are fine.

When you want your amoeba to reproduce, use a unison interval to "divide" your first amoeba. Or divide your amoeba starting with a slow half step up or down trill. Increase the trill speed gradually to full possible speed. Stop the trill, and now the new note is your new amoeba.

Now move your two amoebas independently and chromatically, again with tremolo or vibrato.

If you can play both amoebas simultaneously, go for it!

If you want to create more amoebas, go ahead.

Remember, you have to keep track of them!

At this point, continue with your amoebas, following the conductor's dynamic cues.

To begin the last section, your amoebas will begin to gradually die. An amoeba begins to die when it begins to lose its vibrato or tremolo and gets gradually softer until silence . . . death.

When total silence is achieved, the first movement is completed.

JON: Tim, let's try this first movement.

EZRA: I'm not sure what to do exactly.

TIM: That's understandable, Ezra; I'll write one possible interpretation of "Amoeba Form" in traditional notation on the board, to clarify my concept. Notice the chromatic motion. In bar 6 the first amoeba divides with the trill, and now we have two amoebas moving independently, at first in contrary motion.

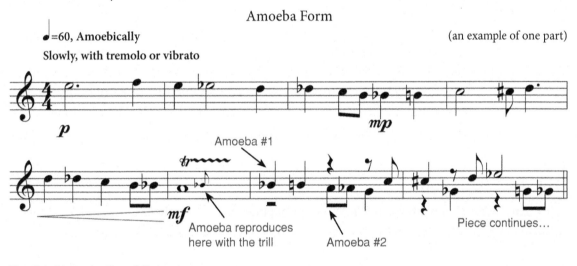

Fig. 8.1. "Amoeba Form" Example

JON: Tim, I'm happy that you're able to bring your conceptual ideas to standard notation like this. This shows that you're beginning to become more flexible in your creative thinking.

TIM: When I tried this piece by myself, it really took some concentration to keep track of the amoebas. I had three going for a bit. I'd like to try it as a duo. Any takers?

MASTY: Sure.

Masty and Tim begin to play and produce a modern, classical-sounding duo variation of "Amoeba Form."

TIM: Thanks, Masty. Now let's try "Amoeba Form" with all of us. Is everyone ready? Start your amoebas!

An incredibly beautiful Webern-like piece transpires.

TIM: Wow, that was pretty intense. I liked it a lot.

JON: Well, Tim, it is your composition.

BRUNO: Just for contrast, let's try doing this with Olympic-level amoebas! Let's do a variation using a traditional scale instead of the chromatic scale so that now the amoebas can at times move by a whole step. Reproduction can still be with a trill, but make the trill sometimes a whole step.

TIM: Bruno, you may not believe this, but my third movement is very similar to this.

BRUNO: Great minds think alike, Tim.

> Just as Tim brought his conceptual "Amoeba Form" opus to traditional notation, how would you "translate" the first movement of "Amoeba Form" into your medium?
>
> I imagine a dance work for four dancers representing one amoeba. They are huddled tightly together, hugging, vibrating slightly, moving as one, in slow motion. They gradually begin to reproduce by splitting into two pairs of huddled, hugging dancers, and then splitting into four solo dancers. Continuing to vibrate and move, they gradually reach an eventual stillness. I can see this dance moving really slowly.

THE GOLDFISH STORY

JON: Another one of my favorite CreW pieces happens to be a Mother Nature–inspired piece. One of your CreW ancestors brought in his pet goldfish to be our conductor for a piece.

CHESTER: No way!

JON: On the side of the goldfish bowl he drew the five lines of a staff, and wherever the fish's snout went we played those notes. For two weeks we were preparing the piece for a concert, and then tragically, the goldfish died!

MASTY: That's too bad.

JON: Not really, Masty. Everything worked out. The deceased goldfish's understudy did a great job.

Some of the zaniest Creative Workshop ideas seem to work the best. They help us to become childlike again, stirring up curiosity, an important ingredient in creative endeavors.

The goldfish story also inspired a dance, this time a solo dance improvisation. Project the goldfish and bowl onto several large video monitors set around a stage and have a solo ballerina mimic the motions of the goldfish. How about a bevy of ballerinas? I really wish I knew a good "How many ballerinas does it take to change a lightbulb" joke right now!

Wait—I have one.

How many ballerinas does it take to change a lightbulb?

Give up? Two. One ballerina to hold the lightbulb while on point, and a second ballerina gently pushing her elbow to get her spinning.

"BEEBOP"

JON: So, CreW, how did your snow crystal scratchboard project work out?

TIM: When I worked on my scratchboard, I was spellbound by the beauty of the snowflake photos and the possibilities it presented. I also read the Gyorgy Doczi book *The Power of Limits* that you suggested. It illustrates the hexagonal shape that many snowflakes have in common. I started thinking about other incredible natural designs found in leaves, flowers, and insects. How do bees make those perfect looking hexagons? Then I thought, what does it sound like in that honeycomb?

JON: Wow, Tim, the snow crystal really inspired you. From snowflakes to bee sounds—a nice connection.

TIM: So can we have the workshop produce the sound of hundreds of bees? Let's imagine we are inside the beehive for a while, and then the bees decide to leave the hive and forage for nectar. When the last bee leaves, the piece is ended.

JON: Nice idea, Tim. Would you like to conduct?

TIM: Sure. Imagine the sound intensity inside the hive for a moment. We can jump right into playing that intensity on my downbeat. On my next cue, the bees begin to gradually leave the hive. Ready. On my downbeat.

The workshop plays quite industriously here. Guitarists with all ten fingers tapping away on their strings, horns and voices scatting beelike sounds, and gradually the hive empties out to silence.

JON: So now we have the birds *and* the bees. What next, nature lovers?

TIM: Oh, by the way, I call this piece "BeeBop."

JON: Ouch, and badda-boom!

"TREES #1"

CHESTER: I have a revelation, and a thank you for the workshop. In the first several weeks of this class, I realized that I had some serious writer's block. Ideas avoided me like the plague. Now, after hearing and playing CreW ideas for a couple of months, I feel less directly responsible to be creative. I feel that I can draw creative energy from elements all around me.

JON: I like the way you're thinking, Chester.

CHESTER: Thank you, CreW. So, I have my first piece today.

JON: Fire away!

CHESTER: I really like harmony and chords, and I realize that chords have roots, and so do trees. Trees have an annual cycle of growing leaves and losing leaves. So why not have everyday chords be inspired by this incredible cycle? This is a simple piece for one person playing a chord or an activated arpeggio. Anyone can do this on a piano, by the way. I sketched this piece out for everyone.

Readers, go right ahead and try this piece. Go find that piano again! Use any notes you wish to create your tree.

Trees #1:
Summer to Fall

Choose any five- or six-note chord structure. Think of this as a tree.

The chord's bottom or lowest note is the root of the tree.

All the other notes are the leaves of the tree.

Play the chord (your tree) and generally sustain this sound in your own way.

Think of yourself as the wind moving the tree (chord) all at once, or just have some of the leaves move by themselves.

At your discretion, autumn arrives and the leaves of the tree will slowly fade and fall to the ground, in the following manner:

Make a leaf (a note of the chord) fall by repeating one of the chord's notes loudly at first, then softer and softer until the leaf disappears into silence.

Continue in this manner until all the leaves (notes) have fallen from your tree (chord).

JON: That looks like a fun piece, Chester. Can we hear your solo interpretation?

Chester plays a brief version of "Trees #1."

CHESTER: I am happy to say that it felt perfectly natural for me to conceive of and play this piece. I would have thought of this as pretty weird a few weeks ago. Now I have ideas for more tree studies that I'll use to compose a piece for string quartet written in traditional notation.

Fellow artists, I hope you are drawing inspiration from the workshop. It's working for Chester! I must have been a dancer in a former life, because I'm seeing Chester's "Trees #1: Summer to Fall" inspiring a nice choreography.

"HOME ON THE RANGE" AND "BIRD OPUS"

BRUNO: How can I use this Mother Nature stuff on a gig?

JON: A great question, Bruno. Actually, if you're talking about making money, I could imagine Tim's "Amoeba Study" as a nice premise for a movie theme! I composed a piece for Greenpeace that uses prepared, prerecorded Mother Nature sounds and some quodlibet. I use wolf vocalizations as a backdrop for the traditional song "Home on the Range." The wolf sounds add a powerful dimension to the theme. I performed and recorded this piece as a duet with Bill Frisell and, commercially speaking, the audience loved it!

I also use prerecorded material of bird songs and calls in a work titled "Bird Opus." In this piece the performers play along with the recording and follow a guide sheet that describes the progression of bird sounds on the recording. This enables the performers to anticipate an upcoming sound. The accompanying recording begins with the impressive song of the Common Loon, followed by its tremolo call. The "lead sheet" for "Bird Opus" reads like this:

A long clean medium-loud glissando_____fast, louder shaking attacks.

"Bird Opus" continues with a variety of bird sounds. In a recording of "Bird Opus" it's difficult to tell the avian sounds from the Homo sapiens sounds!!

Drawing and Traditional Notation Improvisations

CreW and readers, please get out your pencils. Here is a very simple four-line poem inspired by Mother Nature that I wrote this past week during a trip to Maine. I will read it a few times. I would like each of you to make a sketch, a doodle perhaps, or use traditional notation to express an improvisation inspired by the poem. I have provided a blank bit of manuscript paper and a blank bit of "canvas" for you. You have exactly three minutes. Here goes. Remember to let your reactions flow unfettered.

> Unfettered feathers rising above the quiet pond
> A bird's laughter, then a dive for dinner
> As a raven shows interest with his guttural call
> the eagle flies by, caring less

CreW and readers, your blank manuscript and canvas are right here. Give it a try for about three minutes.

Fig. 8.2. Reader's Manuscript and Canvas

JON: All right, everyone, time's up. How did everyone do?

MASTY: Here's mine.

TIM: And mine.

JON: Masty and Tim, let's take a look at yours.

Fig. 8.3. Masty's and Tim's Poetry Examples

JON: Quite a contrast here, a statement for flute and one for double bass.

MASTY: I heard this simple flute melody as you read your poem. It is a pretty blatant text painting, I suppose.

JON: Nice job, Masty.

TIM: I kept mine simple.

JON: Right, Tim. Both of these statements are perfect reactions to the poem. I want all of you to work on feeling as comfortable improvising with pencil and paper as with your imaginations and instruments.

TIM: Jon, the reader didn't sketch in an improv to your poem.

JON: Perhaps they didn't like my poem.

TIM: No, I think the reader is just using silence space *very* efficiently!

JON: That must be it!

ALEX'S "STELLA BY BLINKLIGHT"

JON: Here is a brilliant Mother Nature piece conceived by Alex, a Creative Workshop ancestor, that is inspired by the human body. This piece calls upon one of our essential bodily rhythms, blinking. Simply, the blink of a player's eyes acts as an inner conductor. Alex had the workshop play the standard song "Stella by Starlight." Each player was assigned to play either the tune's melody line or chord accompaniment. On cue, the workshop began and the blink of each player's eyes conducted that player when to play the next melody note or chord. Using blinking as an inner conductor is a fascinating technique that produced a selfless, natural, beautiful, shimmering rhythmic ambience. Thank you, Alex.

How could you tap into blinking rhythm in your work? Imagine if the pointillist Seurat used this technique. He'd still be painting! How about having two or more dancers move through a series of ten postures, each dancer conducted by their inner blink to indicate movement to the next posture. Or possibly a scene in a theater piece could use some "blink" timing! How about an entire theater piece moving by blinks, perhaps a minimalist, Samuel Beckett–inspired work!

NEXT WEEK'S THEME

JON: Take a look in a mirror at one of the most remarkable products of Mother Nature, you! Homo sapiens, bearer of an ancient instrument, the human voice. Let's use our oral imaginations and explore the vocal sounds within and outside of our language. The vocal sounds in the sentences I am speaking now are certainly familiar, but what about some of these words I am creating on the board?

Snull garnth yuj choola binta fivatik

JON: Anyone wish to add to the possibilities? Come right up, Masty.

lesyor tuk nij yoonte ladinth gup olip

JON: Nice ones, Masty. Got some more, Yuto? Come right up.

pidge mik tunch flim ast yok shnootz

JON: Those are lovely. I don't think any of those exist in the English language. Do any of those "words" exist in the Japanese language, Yuto?

YUTO: I don't think so.

JON: How about in Spanish, Roberto?

ROBERTO: Nope, but I am not sure how they should be pronounced.

JON: That's a good point Roberto, and reminds me of the many sound possibilities that our voices can produce! In fact our topic for next week is Playing an Ancient Instrument: The Human Voice, the world's most powerful instrument.

CreW, before we close up, let's find a few more chords for our "Democratic Chorale." We started it back in our second week of class.

> Readers, if you would like to hear how the birds have inspired a master composer, give a listen to "Le Merle Noir" (The Black Thrush). Olivier Messiaen composed this duet for piano and flute.

CHAPTER 9 – WEEK 9
PLAYING AN ANCIENT INSTRUMENT: THE HUMAN VOICE

Creativity is contagious. Pass it on. —Albert Einstein

JON: Good day, everyone. We have used the power of the human voice in our first week's meeting with Sprecht-Blots, and in "The Village." I even gave a political speech, and read a few of my bad poems!

MASTY: I like your poetry, Jon.

JON: Why thank you, Masty. The sensuality of using our voices and the sympathetic response of our bodies to other voices are two powerful reasons to explore this ancient instrument further.

EZRA: Why do you refer to your voice as ancient, Jon? You don't look that old.

Some chuckles emanate from the workshop.

JON: Ezra, our voices connect us to our ancient ancestors, the inventors of spoken language, considered to be one of humankind's greatest inventions. In week one I presented an imagined story in which an early cave hunter used an excited *AAAAOOOORAHRRH* and *BOOMMMPH* to vocally describe to his cave mates his capture of a woolly mammoth. Now, millions of years later, our voices can still produce those same sounds. We still have the same instrument consisting of our diaphragm, voice box, throat, tongue, and lips. Then throw in body gestures for dramatic effect. Wow! One of the first sounds we heard while growing in our mother's womb was our parents' excited, loving voices. What a powerful connection.

Another powerful connection to our spoken language is the ability to capture these sounds visually with our written language, another incredible human invention.

Do you think hand gestures were humankind's first visual language? That language still thrives today in the lively dance of hand gestures in a conversation on a street in Rome. Were the early cave-paintings—storytelling with paintings—a predecessor to written language? Some early cave paintings are quite representational, with a horned animal being pursued by bow-and-arrow-bearing humans. Was this visual story gradually simplified down to essential strokes to inspire visual language, the animal down to two inward-curving strokes—its horns—and the hunter symbolized with a diagonal arrow-tipped line? These paintings, along with early rock sculptures, reflect a very high intelligence.

Speaking of incredible prehistoric sculpture, recently a 35,000-year-old flute carved from a vulture bone was discovered in a German cave. The flute has five holes and a notched mouthpiece—the oldest instrument discovery on record.

Let's imagine that we are early cave peoples inventing early visual language. How would you, as a cave person, represent essential elements in everyday cave life with a simple shape or symbol?

How would you represent the following words with shapes, using pen and paper?

mother   fire   water   birth   death   baby   rain

Now, what *sound* do you imagine the early cave people gave to these symbols you have created?

A Scat Singing Session: Great Therapy!

JON: Please look at the board for a moment.

TIM: Yikes! Some more of your invented words Jon?

JON: No, these are right from a dictionary.

hame oowee reet skiffle cack blip zanzy goola eel-ya-dah

TIM: From what language?

JON: I used Robert Gold's book *A Jazz Lexicon* to find those words. Here is a sentence: "Got a blip for 'ya bruz?" Which means, "Do you have a nickel, brother?" If you notice, all the words feel good to say, and sound cool as well.

BRUNO: "Eel-ya-dah" sounds like scat syllables.

JON: Good, Bruno. "Eel-ya-dah" is a representation of the triplet figure common in bebop.

Class, just for a warm-up, let's do some scat singing. Will someone please play a simple blues accompaniment? Thanks, Yuto. Please do not feel obligated to sing, though I do feel that singing, along with dancing, gives us a closer understanding of the power of music by using our bodies as an instrument.

Most of CreW gives scatting a try.

JON: Do you notice that each of us has our own personal vocabulary of seemingly nonsense syllables that makes perfect sense to us?

BRUNO: You're right, Jon, it feels good to sing and use certain syllables. I like the "B" ones.

Fellow artists, forget the illusion that you are not a singer. Start scat singing right now. What scat syllables feel good to you? Sing something bluesy and find out! Scat singing is therapeutic. No matter what your artistic medium, developing a regular diet of scat singing will inspire and massage your creative spirit. Think of scat singing as meditative, a "running mantra." Close your eyes and start scatting. You are the conductor—any syllables are fine, any rhythms or pitches are fine. Just start scatting, observing what feels good. If something doesn't feel good just let it go by and KEEP SCATTING!! Yes, after the shower, keep scatting. Internally, silently, keep scatting. Let the scatting massage your mind, your chest, your soul. Soft scat, loud scat, tight-mouthed scat, loose-mouthed scat, silent scat, deep in your mind scat, the entire body and soul vibrates when scatting, from the tip to the top, tip, top, tip, top, tip, tip, tip, top, tip, tip, tip, tipity, tipity, topity. Tip! Hey it was fun working from the letter T. How about the letter B? bip, bop, bopity, bam, bam bingle.

Try scatting on the keyboard.

You say that's gibberish? Find your special gibberish. Scatting is akin to doodling, subconscious sketching.

BRUNO'S "INDIAN MUSIC SYLLABLES"

BRUNO: In Indian music class we use scatlike syllables to create rhythmic groupings. Here is a really nice one for a group of nine.

Bruno writes it on the board.

ta ka di mi ta ka ta ki ta

BRUNO: When you mentioned exploring with voice last week, this voice technique came to mind, and I created this quartet. I use some Indian syllables along with some of my own. It's fairly minimalist. Each line is spoken and repeated.

ka-tik-a-tik   ka-tik-a-tik   ka-tik-a-tik   ka-tik-a-tam

shloomapalapa   shloomapaluja

cha   chachacha   cha   chachacha   cha   chachacha

ooooomapatikva   lapa   chacha   shloomapalaka

Fig. 9.1. Bruno's "Indian Music Syllables"

JON: Let's try it. Bruno, please say the first line to give us a basic tempo.

Bruno suggests a fairly quick tempo.

JON: Roberto and Bruno, take the top line, Masty and Tim the second line, Ezra and Chester the third line, and Yuto and I will scat the bottom line. Does this have to rhythmically stay together, Bruno?

BRUNO: No, but each line should maintain its starting tempo and groove. On my downbeat . . . ready . . . go.

MASTY: Wow, I apologize but it's hard not to laugh!

BRUNO: That's okay, Masty, they're tricky, and we *are* moving pretty fast. One more time . . . ready . . . go.

JON: That is a nice effect, Bruno. I feel that these mantralike syllables should be delivered more slowly and repeated many times, gradually building to an intensity. I am hearing a group of monks singing this in a beautiful setting.

LANGUAGE IS AN IMPRESSIVE MUSIC!

JON: Just to show you folks what a great instrument your voice is, check this out. How many of you do transcribing—listening to and writing down musical ideas?

Several hands shoot up.

JON: Who feels that they are really good at it?

Yuto's hand shoots up again.

JON: Okay, Yuto. Grab a pencil and manuscript paper. Let me give you a middle C from the piano for a relative pitch. I have something for you to transcribe.

I begin speaking.

JON: Hi. My name is Jon Damian and I am from Brooklyn, New York. Did you know that Brooklyn is the fourth largest city in the United States, and is known as the city of churches?

YUTO: You want me to transcribe your speaking voice?

JON: Yes, Yuto.

YUTO: When you speak, you are using too many pitches, quarter tones and stuff; they won't fit on the music staff.

JON: All right then, let me put the metronome on at 60 BPM. *Click . . . Click . . .* Now Yuto, transcribe the rhythms of my speaking.

As a child I found Brooklyn to be filled with fascinating places, and people. One of my fondest memories was eating potato knishes at Coney Island beach . . .

Yuto interrupts.

YUTO: It is very difficult. The rhythms are too complex to transcribe. In your speaking voice the gradations of pitches and rhythms are much finer than in music.

JON: Exactly, Yuto. The pitches and rhythms we produce are really cool. We are all strongly attached to language. It helps us to get our own way, buy a pizza, and to effectively argue with our significant others. Most important, using language is a highly developed improvisational ability. I wish my jazz improvisation was as powerful as my improvisation with language.

"KUBLA KHAN"

How would you translate the unique, creative richness of the rhythms, pitches, and articulations of your voice into your medium? Please read aloud the beginning of "Kubla Khan," a poem by Samuel Taylor Coleridge.

Kubla Khan
In Xanadu did Kubla Khan
A stately pleasure dome decree
Where Alph, the sacred river, ran
Through caverns measureless to man
Down to a sunless sea.

Read the verse again a few times, and very lightly, silently, clap your hands together with the rhythm of your voice. Next, try it again, allowing the rest of your body to be inspired to dance. Now try reading and pencil sketching on paper in the poem's rhythms and to the words of the poem. Your pencil is not unlike a drumstick attacking the skin of a drum. Do the poem's rhythms act as a catalyst for your sketching hand? Let the various round and sharp syllable sounds inspire your pencil's attack. Remember, we have a lot of creative ability with delivering our spoken language. We can make, or break, a person's heart with it!

"DOREEN AND ALICE"

JON: One of my earliest avant-garde compositions, "Doreen and Alice," was inspired by spoken language. This piece was essentially sung-spoke to me by someone I have never seen or met.

A hand goes up. "How could that be?"

JON: As a student back in the late 1960s I rented a room in Sally's Rooming House at 81 Westland Avenue in Boston's Back Bay for forty-eight dollars a month. Need I say, simple accommodations?

Late one evening while I was meditating, an anonymous voice called out inquisitively from the back alleyway beneath my window, "Do-re-en?" After several more seconds, again, louder, "Do-re-en?" And then a third time, stronger still, "Do-re-en?!" Followed by a quick, louder, "A-lice?!" Intrigued, I peered from my window. I saw nothing, but quickly scratched down this verbal scenario.

I go to the whiteboard.

Do-re-en?

Do-re-en?

Do-re-en?!

A-lice?!

JON: The simple form intrigued me—a statement of a name, repetition of the name, then a contrasting name. This mysterious voice gave me the seeds for an interesting form for improvisation. I was fortunate at the time to be a member of a new music ensemble, an early creative workshop, to whom I introduced "Doreen and Alice." The motifs are clear: two names, one name of three syllables, the other name of two syllables; one name of a warm articulation tone color, the other of a bright articulation tone color. "Doreen and Alice" works for an ensemble of one or more participants.

EZRA: I've heard "Doreen and Alice" on your *Dedications: Faces and Places* CD. It sounds great with your Rubbertellie. I like how you used your voice with the instrument and hybridized the names creating "Al-len" and "Dor-is"! Can you bring your Rubbertellie in to show us how it works?

JON: Sure, Ezra.

So let's try a group version of "Doreen and Alice." Remember to play—vocalize the head twice, as together as possible, using your voices and instruments simultaneously, if possible, and then improvise. On cue a final statement of the head, ending on an extended "A-lice!?" . . . Ready? All together, and begin.

The workshop enjoys using their voices here.

JON: Playing with the groups of twos and threes and the tone colors of the syllables created by the names helped a lot; the motifs are really clear.

Several years after composing "Doreen and Alice" I created a choreography for a solo dance to be performed along with the piece. The solo dancer portrays two dear old friends. Alice is represented by the dancer's actual face and Doreen is represented by a Japanese Noh mask attached to the back of the dancer's head. Doreen suffers from Alzheimer's disease. The piece begins with opening statements, Alice calling out to Doreen three times, with no response until a frantic response from Doreen: "Alice?!" with a turn of the dancer's head exposing the Noh mask to the audience. The dancer's improvisation unfurls from here. The only props are the mask, a rocking chair, a lamp, a simple costume, and a ball of yarn stuffed into the dancer's sweater pocket. As the dance proceeds, eventually the yarn begins to unwind, wrapping around the dancer like some evil cocoon, slowly consuming the dancer. Not a very cheerful piece, but a powerful one.

TIM'S TONGUE TWISTERS

TIM: Jon, is this a good time to try my tongue twister idea?

JON: Thank you for your patience, Tim. Go right ahead.

Tim comes to the front of the room.

TIM: In the English language we have tongue twisters, and I had a thought. Do other languages have them also?

JON: Great question. Let's ask our international colleagues. Yuto, are there tongue twisters in the Japanese language?

YUTO: What is a tongue twister?

JON: A tongue twister is a tricky to say series of words. Something like . . .

YUTO: Oh, I know what you mean! In Japanese we have many. Here is my favorite one. I'll say it and then write it phonetically on the board.

Sumomo mo momo momo mo momo sumomo mo momo mo momo no uchi.

JON: Wow, that's cool, Yuto. What does it mean?

YUTO: The translation is "A Japanese plum is a kind of peach, a peach is also a peach, both Japanese plum and peach are kinds of peaches."

ROBERTO: Check this out, this is a Spanish tongue twister.

JON: Write it up there, Roberto.

ROBERTO: Remember to roll those letter *R*'s.

Rosa Rizo resa ruso, ruso reza Rosa Rizo.

ROBERTO: It means, "Rosa Rizo prays in Russian, in Russian prays Rosa Rizo." But here is my favorite because it sounds like what it is saying! Well sort of. First the translation.

I enter a train with wheat with you, a train with wheat I enter with you.

Here it is in español. Let me say it. Those rolled letter *R*'s are again really important here.

Contigo entro un tren con trigo un tren con trigo contigo entro.

ROBERTO: Do you think it sounds like a train?

JON: It sure does, and what a nice tongue twister, Roberto.

CHESTER: The beauty of spoken language becomes more apparent when I hear a language I don't speak. I can't get caught up in the meaning of the words.

JON: That's a good point, Chester. Yes, Masty?

MASTY: Can anyone do this Persian tongue twister? You have to repeat it as fast as possible.

> Sheikh Saadi sakht shakhsi
> Sheikh Saadi sakht shakhsi
> Sheikh Saadi sakht shakhsi

JON: Thank you for these great twisters. CreW, here is an English twister you have to repeat, also as fast as possible.

> Eleven benevolent elephants
> Eleven benevolent elephants
> Eleven benevolent elephants

TIM: So how can we make music with these tongue twisters?

JON: These twisters are already quite musical and have simple compositional integrity. They have repetition of syllable sounds and some even have a point of contrasting syllable sound, as in Yuto's twister, *momo . . . uchi*. Repetition and contrast, the magic formula.

TIM: Can we try bringing some of these twisters together as duets? We can vocally scat *these tumbling tense twisters textures tumbling together!*

JON: Yeah, Tim. Nice one.

EZRA'S "FROM CHAOS TO FOCUS"

EZRA: I have a quartet voice piece.

JON: Lay it on us, Ezra.

EZRA: It's sort of a surprise, but I want to hear the effect of the piece as well. I have four different parts for the workshop to read at the same time. Think proportional notation, and with each repetition shorten the silence between syllables bit by bit. We can only play this piece once for full effect.

Ezra directs the workshop here.

EZRA: Okay, workshop colleagues. Read the syllables in a basic speaking voice, and again, diminish the silence space at each repeat. Ready, everyone . . . go!

Readers, join in and read. Here is one of the parts for Ezra's voice piece. Remember to repeat it, and bring the syllables closer together each time.

```
TH   EC   REA
TI   VEW   OR
KSH   OPI   SMY
FAVO   RI   TE   CLAS
SJO   NDAM   I   A
NIS   A   NAB   SOL
UT   EGE   N   IUS
```

The workshop begins, and as Ezra predicted, gradually the piece gels and CreW has a nice laugh.

JON: That was very nice of you, Ezra, and a very nice effect.

EZRA: I'm glad you liked it, Jon, and that it worked out as I hoped. I call the concept "From Chaos to Focus," and I will try this with various texts. I am trying to develop an extended traditionally notated piece that works from the same premise.

Ezra's voice piece idea is, in a sense, a cubist view of written language. The essentials are broken up, changing the original view of the words, which at first look ambiguous and then gradually come into focus.

Take an old painting. One that you have really never been happy with—there must be one! Slice it up, put the parts together cubistically. How about building a mobile with them?

JON: Hopefully, CreW, after today's session you will not hear the human voice in quite the same way again. In fact, if you wish to hear another dimension of using the incredible human voice, check out the throat singers of Tuva, near Mongolia. One singer sings two parts simultaneously, creating counterpoint. Great stuff.

ASSIGNMENT FOR WEEK 10

JON: So, CreW, let's shut our mouths for a while and try another resource to get those creative juices flowing. See what inspiration you can draw from inanimate everyday objects found around the house. Yep, from soup to nuts, throw in the kitchen sink if you wish. Lamps, colanders, spoons, open up that chock-filled drawer and scrounge around. Toothpicks, jars of marmalade, vacuum cleaners. Use these found objects as inspirational material. Our homes are filled with incredible creations. Check out *1001 Inventions That Changed the World* by Jack Challoner. Thanks to this book I discovered that the button was invented around 3000 BCE! More than fifty designs were created and patented in the search for the most efficient way to clip sheets of paper together. The flat-bottomed paper bag was invented by Margaret Knight, one of the first American women to be awarded a patent. Take a look at the histories of nails, coat hangers, tape, and staplers. Very inspirational objects!

See you next week.

CHAPTER 10 – WEEK 10
EVERYDAY OBJECTS YOU FIND AROUND THE HOUSE

It's a common word, something you'd find around the house.

—Groucho Marx

FOUND OBJECT PIECES

JON: Today's theme was inspired by this quote from the great Groucho Marx, the leader of the Marx brothers comedy troupe. Groucho's TV game show *You Bet Your Life* had a secret word segment introduced with the line, "It's a common word, something you'd find around the house." If anyone said the secret word during the show, they would win a nice pile of cash.

AZ: Good morning, Jon! Bruno has a gig, and he called me a few days ago to fill in for him.

JON: Nice to see you again, Az.

To continue with Groucho's inspiration, how did everyone do with the assignment? Yuto?

YUTO'S "STRING OPUS"

YUTO: I found a ball of string and, being a visual artist as well as a musician, I produced some paintings with the string. I cut a length of string, dipped it in ink, and pulled it out, letting the excess ink drip back into the bottle. I held the inked string vertically over a piece of paper and slowly lowered the string towards the paper, painting with the string. Then I carefully pulled the string up and away from the paper to complete the work. I selected my favorites from many I had made. I also created an improvisational opus for solo guitar based on the paintings. Would you like to see one of the paintings?

Readers, Yuto's "String Opus" is on the next page.

JON: It's beautiful, Yuto. I can see that using a string as a "brush" works nicely.

YUTO: Thank you, Jon. For my string-inspired opus I capture the essence of an unbroken length of string by playing in a sliding, unbroken manner on a single length of guitar string. I begin by playing a very set series of slides in a repetitive manner, something like this.

Yuto slides around the guitar string for a moment.

YUTO: After a while I let myself become totally free with the slide, building in intensity. A final sustained note, a simple fade out with the slide, marks the ending. It is a simple piece.

JON: I like its simplicity, inspired by a simple object, a string.

Fig. 10.1. Yuto's "String Opus"

Watercolor and oil painters, how about creating a painting done with one brush stroke, never lifting the brush from the paper or canvas until the brush dries. Doing a series in this manner may be interesting, the thread being the one-stroke brush technique. I tried some doodles with one unbroken pen stroke and found some new doodling ideas!

ROBERTO'S "SEPTET FOR SEVEN MUSIC STANDS"

ROBERTO: I just had an idea right now, not with objects found around the house but with objects found here in the classroom—our music stands. Listen to this.

Roberto proceeds to twist with both hands the top section of his black metal music stand, creating a variety of squeaky, sliding sounds, not unpleasant.

ROBERTO: I know this sounds crazy, but can we try a "Septet for Seven Music Stands?"

JON: Roberto, remember that the workshop is our laboratory, so experimentation is a good thing. Any more details?

ROBERTO: How about a simple rondo form? Let's move around the room first with short music stand solos and then begin to overlap until we are all playing together. Next, slowly move back to distinct solos again, becoming shorter and shorter until they essentially disappear. I will conduct.

Roberto's "Septet for Seven Music Stands" produces many new harmonic possibilities.

A FOUND MUSIC BOX

I once discovered an old music box at my Aunt Julie's house, and found it magical and inspirational. It inspired this idea for a simple piece I call "The Music Box."

Imagine anything, anyone, anyplace, as a music box with an imaginary dancer resting on top. Now insert and crank an imaginary key. What do you hear? What do you see? Can you sing it? play it? dance it?

In the world of visual art, inspiration from found objects is a well-worn technique. "Assemblage" is a visual art technique in which three-dimensional works are produced using found objects, also called "readymades." Prime examples are Marcel Duchamp's early twentieth-century works *Bicycle Wheel* (1915), and *Fountain* (1917), which uses a found urinal as its foundation.

I lovingly include this quote from my son Gene, an artist in his own right, whose medium is charcoal on found wood.

You take the ordinary and you point at it. —Eugene Damian

EZRA: Jon, I have a found objects piece to share.

JON: Go right ahead, Ezra.

EZRA'S "RUBBER-BAND BAND"

EZRA: It's a simple idea. These are objects, rubber bands, I found right around my house, on the sidewalk. It's amazing how many I have found on the ground in the neighborhood where I live.

JON: Those rubber bands are from the mail carrier, who tosses them as she delivers the mail.

EZRA: So they're "perks" from the federal government?

JON: I guess you can say that. So how do you want to use these rubber bands?

EZRA: I will give a pile of rubber bands to each of us to create a rubber band instrument. Then we can have a rubber-band band jam.

JON: Great idea!

> This reminds me of another of my fantasies. I would like to film a documentary of a Creative Workshop Ensemble weekend at my cabin in Maine. One of the weekend's activities would be to build pieces and instruments from objects found in and around the woods and river. Then we would exhibit the works and listen to the instrument inventions, a very self-sufficient event.

"THE COMPUTER TUNE"

JON: A number of years ago, when I was a composition student, a teacher was discussing computer-generated music. He played some incredible music generated by the multimillion-dollar computers of the 1950s, notably the 1957 "Illiac Suite" by Leharen Hiller, inspired by a computer of the same name. As a student in the early 1970s, I had no access to these computers. Serendipitously, a few days after the computer music lecture, I found three computer punch cards scattered on the sidewalks of Kenmore Square. Back then these thin, cardboard hole-punched cards were used to input data to computers. Curious, I picked the cards up and, after studying them for a while, came up with an idea for a computer-driven—or should I say, computer-inspired—piece. I noticed that two of the cards were similar. The third card was quite different. So I thought, ABA' (A prime), a simple rondo form. I taped the cards together, placed them flat on a piece of paper, and spray-painted the cards. When I lifted them up, the image you see here remained.

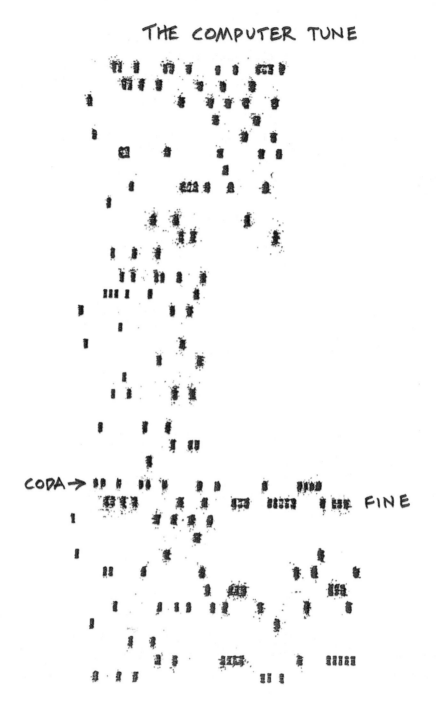

Fig. 10.2. Jon's "Computer Tune"

JON: I brought my new computer tune to my fellow avant-garde music explorers in the Rubbertellie String Quartet, one of the first creative workshop ensembles I led. I told them to imagine the electronic innards of a computer—teeny, mysterious-looking, plastic, soldered gizmos that make mysterious-sounding metal, soldered sounds. The spray-painted computer card images trigger the rhythms for the piece, as in proportional notation. I played the first line of the computer tune for my comrades in a sprightly tempo, working my Rubbertellie assiduously with a metal slide.

zivit zivit   zivit   zivit zivit   zivit   zivit   zivit   zivitzivitzivit   zivit
zivit zivit   zivit   zivit   zivit   zivit   zivit

JON: Then we tried the piece as a group, entering canonically. Player one began to play at the top of the page, player two a bit later, and so forth through the ensemble. "The Computer Tune" was an immediate success, a graphically clear, rhythmic, improvisatory vehicle. Let's play it. First find your own mysterious-sounding, plastic, soldered-sounding sound. Let's start at the right here with Az. When he completes the first line, then Tim begins, and so forth. The first two lines are most important. Keep the intensity building throughout. You can be relaxed with the interpretation of the cards' divots, just keep building. Let it go where it wants to go.

After a serious rendition of "The Computer Tune" a reaction emerges.

CHESTER: Wow, that was intense!

JON: Glad you enjoyed it, Chester. That is my economy plan computer-generated piece.

Fellow artists, "The Computer Tune" is quite a pointillistic piece. I would love to have the great impressionist Georges Seurat jam with the workshop!

GAMES PEOPLE PLAY
"THE TELEPHONE GAME VARIATIONS"

AZ: I was visiting my family over the weekend, and I was thinking about today's theme. A pile of games attracted my attention—Monopoly, Clue, Scrabble—and I thought, would a game make an interesting premise for a piece? What would be the simplest game to build a piece with? All I could think of was some of the parlor games we played at parties, like Charade, Pictionary, and Gossip, the Telephone Game.

JON: This sounds like it has great potential, Az. Continue, please.

AZ: So I chose the Telephone Game.

EZRA: I don't remember this Telephone Game. What are the rules?

AZ: A brief story is taken from a newspaper or magazine. Player one whispers the story into the ear of player two, who whispers what they remember to player three, until everyone has a turn. As the story travels it mutates. Words change in meaning and number. Often the final story barely resembles the original. The final player states their version of the story to the group. Player one reads the original story. The comparisons prove how gossip develops quickly. For a music version of the Telephone Game I have written an original four-bar phrase of music. I will show it to Roberto for ten seconds. He will write down what he remembers. Roberto then holds up his four bars for Tim to see for ten seconds. He writes down what he remembers, and this continues. When each player has completed their part, we can listen to the natural variations of the original theme.

Here is the four-bar phrase. You have ten seconds to look at it, Roberto. Then write down what you remember. Then Tim, you look at Roberto's possibility followed by Ezra, Chester, and Yuto.

Here is the original phrase followed by each workshop member's recollection of the previous phrase.

The Telephone Game Variations

Fig. 10.3. "The Telephone Game Variations"

JON: That's a really nice set of variations. They would sound great played directly through, or as a sextet. There are some very hip canon ideas from part to part.

Try the Telephone Game with several artist friends. Have each artist privately find a simple drawing, and put them all in a box. Have someone begin by choosing one of the sketches, peek at the sketch for ten seconds, then sketch what they remember. This sketch is then shown to the next artist, again for ten seconds, who then completes their sketch from what they remember. Continue, until each artist has completed their sketch. How does the original image evolve through the minds and memories of the artists?

JON: Let's brainstorm some other game possibilities.

SPIN-THE-BOTTLE DUETS

EZRA: Does anyone remember the Spin-the-Bottle game?

Who can forget Spin-the-Bottle!

JON: How can we apply this to music, Ezra?

EZRA: First, let's sit more in a complete circle. One person spins a bottle. When the bottle points at another person, those two play a duet. Then that person spins for a duo-playing partner. If the bottle points to the spinner, the spinner plays a solo. If it lands between two players, those two players play a trio improvisation with the spinner.

JON: Great idea, Ezra. An aleatoric orchestrator!

> Spin-the-Bottle is a nice chance-operated device. Have the spinning bottle choose colors, words, dance poses. Perhaps that bottle will break a creative block. Aleatoric technique is fun to experiment with. If you don't like the result, you can always blame chance!

CHARADES VARIATIONS

TIM: How about Charades? Each player writes down a well-known tune title on a piece of paper to put in a hat. I pick a tune out of the hat. At the downbeat, using my body silently, as in Charades, I give clues. The first to *play* the opening phrase of the tune correctly wins. My fingers will indicate the number of words in the tune title.

Tim picks his first title. He holds up one finger, a one-word tune title. Then he holds up one finger again. Quite quickly Az begins to play the tune "One" from *A Chorus Line.*

AZ: That was easy. I played that show with my high school theater group.

TIM: Okay, Az. Here's another one.

Tim holds up two fingers. Then he points upward, makes a large circular gesture with his arms, and mops his brow with his hand. Az responds, playing the opening melody of "Sunrise Sunset."

TIM: You are fast, Az. Okay. One more folks.

Tim holds up seven fingers, and then makes a gesture that he is standing at bat at home plate.

EZRA: "Take Me Out To The Ball Game"!

TIM: Ezra, you must *play* the tune with your instrument.

EZRA: Oh right, sorry, Tim.

TIM: And the notes have to be right.

JON: CreW, those were some nice possibilities, and Tim, thanks for your game idea.

> All these workshop game ideas would be fun to try with your own music and art and dance groups. Give them a spin.

THE GAMES OF BROOKLYN

JON: My musical imagination is really bubbling, thinking of all the wonderful games we played as children back home in Brooklyn. They were simple games such as Stoop Ball, Johnny on the Pony, Ring-a-levio, Stick Ball, and of course, good old Tag—so many potential pieces. Thank you for letting me reminisce, and I hope you enjoy thinking about your own childhood games as inspiration for pieces.

ROBERTO'S "SUPER DUPER DOUBLE WHAMMY LEMON PIE"

ROBERTO: Jon, I have an idea that I think will work deliciously.

JON: Okay—let's see if we can bring it to life.

ROBERTO: I like to cook, and my kitchen is filled with a variety of cookbooks. So I chose a recipe for an improvisatory piece. Recipes are so developmental.

Each player is responsible for one or more ingredients. One person reads the recipe and the other players respond. Let's try one of my own recipes. I call it my "Super Duper Double Whammy Lemon Pie." I read the recipe, and you guys improvise. I have assigned ingredients for each of you. Jon, I need you to play. Az, please portray the butter since Bruno is not here. Remember to keep the ingredient motif you initially play throughout the piece, varying it as the recipe suggests. Be as blatant as possible.

Roberto begins to read his recipe, starting with setting up the ingredients motifs.

Ingredients:
A pie shell, pre-baked—Jon
One cup of sugar—Masty
2 tablespoons of baking soda—Ezra
1 cup of water—Yuto
2 beaten egg yolks—Chester
1 tablespoon of lemon peel, grated—Tim
3 tablespoons of lemon juice—Tim
1 tablespoon of butter or margarine—Bruno
2 egg whites—Chester

Preparation:

> First mix the baking soda, and the sugar. Now stir in the water a little at a time. When the consistency is smooth, add in the egg yolks. Boil over a medium heat for about a minute while mixing. Remove from the stove. Now add the grated lemon peel, the lemon juice, and the butter. Pour this mixture into the prebaked pie shell. Beat the egg whites for one minute. Add the sugar and beat until the mixture is stiff. Spread the stiff egg white mixture on the pie. Preheat your oven to 325 degrees. Cook until the crust is brown. Remove from the oven, and cool in the refrigerator until serving.

The workshop has some laughs with this recipe and comes up with some interesting musical interpretations.

MASTY: Wow! Now I'm really hungry.

JON: I love the way the recipe orchestrates the improvisation and feeds levels of intensity.

YOLANDA MEMORIES

JON: Roberto, you must be clairvoyant; I have also used recipes for performance pieces. The recipe for polenta from Marguerite Buonopane's *The North End Union Italian Cookbook* was performed by The Boston New Music Ensemble, another early Creative Workshop Ensemble, at Mobius in Boston. For this piece the ensemble was augmented by our librettist, recipe reader Yolanda LaCroix, a lovely woman who was seventy-eight years old at the time. She read the polenta recipe as the ensemble improvised. My favorite part was when Yolanda couldn't keep a straight face or complete a line without giggling.

The *Cooking Channel* and the reasons for its incredible popularity was the topic on a talk radio show one day. Many possible reasons hit me, like a saucepan on the side of the head! I'm sure many of us can remember being in a nice warm kitchen baking something fattening, like cookies or a birthday cake, creating a strong sensory memory. The sound of the beaters rattling against the bowl, the smells, the tastes, the colors, and the feel of those goodies in our hands and mouths is somehow never far away. Culinary art is an incredible medium, the only art that utilizes *all* the senses and dimensions.

Nice recipe piece, Roberto.

ROBERTO: Thanks, everyone, I'll make some pie for all of you for next week.

> These recipe pieces also work for dance group improvisation as well as drama group pieces. Robert Pasoli's Open Theatre troupe actors portray weapons and colors. Why not a half cup of Parmigiano-Reggiano cheese?

Next Week's Activities

JON: We have some guests coming to work with us next week, so Roberto, please make a little extra pie. And Az, you are invited.

ROBERTO: I'll make plenty of pie. Who are the guests?

JON: We have three guests: Sten Höstfält, a guitarist and former CreW member, will be here with some microtonal music. Yumi, Yuto's friend from The Museum School, is a sculptor. The third guest is a surprise.

As always, new works are welcome. Next week please come in at 8:30 a.m. to give us some time to discuss CreW business before our guests arrive at 9 a.m.

Thanks to Groucho for today's theme!

GUEST ARTISTS WEEK

I don't paint dreams or nightmares, I paint my own reality.—Frida Kahlo

MASTY: Good morning, Jon. Our game-inspired pieces last week got me thinking about one of my favorite childhood games, so I have a traditionally notated dominoes-inspired piece for today.

JON: Masty, we have two guests coming today . . .

EZRA: And a surprise guest?

JON: Yes, Ezra, and a surprise guest. Masty, given our time constraints today, we'll do your dominoes-inspired piece at our session next week.

MASTY: OK, but may I pass out the music now? It's a quartet for woodwinds and pretty slow, but can use a looking at.

JON: Sure. CreW, let's put Masty's piece in our folders for now.

NEXT WEEK'S THEME

JON: Good morning, Az, I'm glad you could join us. Thank you all for coming in earlier this morning. Before our guests arrive, let's discuss next week's theme. Chester, can you please write on the board the five senses.

sight hearing touch taste smell

TIM: What about the sixth sense, somatosensation and extrasensory perception?

JON: Those are fascinating possibilities, but for now, for simplicity's sake, let's consider those other senses heightened forms of our five basic senses.

As we reflect on our activities together this semester, we have been creating and sharing ideas in a range of arts, from acting to quilt making. In these arts, which senses, or what "receptors," do we use as artists and observers?

BRUNO: Our senses of sight and hearing.

JON: Why don't we tap into our senses, our receptors, of touch, taste, and smell to inspire and create our works? Roberto?

ROBERTO: We can't taste, touch, or smell music, or a painting? Actually, I love culinary art since it's the only art medium that does cater to all five senses. I hope that my lemon pie not only looks and tastes and smells great, but also feels and sounds great as we bite into the crunchy crust. You showed us a BluesShape pizza, and I'm sure it tasted and smelled great also, and the sound of that crust!

JON: Great observation. That pizza was a *reaction* to music thinking. Why don't we try using our senses of taste, touch, and smell to act as *triggers* for music ideas? Put your imaginations to work for our next meeting. By the way, Roberto, those pies smell awfully good.

ROBERTO: Thanks, Jon, I made two of my lemon pies. That should be enough for CreW and our guests.

OUR FIRST GUEST: YUMI

YUTO: Good morning, everyone. I'd like to introduce my friend Yumi. She is a student at the Museum School.

YUMI: It is nice to meet everyone.

JON: It looks like you brought a lot of supplies.

YUMI: Thanks to Yuto's help, I could bring my entire setup—my sculpting tools, sculpting table, and a nice block of clay.

JON: Yumi, have you ever worked with other kinds of artists before?

YUMI: I have worked along with other sculptors on large projects, but never with artists of other media. I am nervous.

JON: Yumi, in the Creative Workshop, we are here to be inspired by each other and offer support. Hopefully there will be a nice mix of communication from medium to medium.

YUMI: I will sculpt with clay as you sculpt with sound, and we can inspire each other.

JON: Great. Before we begin, CreW, as you play, maintain a focus on Yumi's sculpting and sculpture as reference points. Don't let your playing distract you from this visual interchange. Yuto?

Yuto begins to play, setting up a nice sound ambience for Yumi, who seems receptive and begins to work her clay with her hands. CreW begins to react to Yuto and Yumi, and slowly the workshop and sculptor are on their way. CreW gets excited quickly, Yumi follows suit, grabs some tools, and pushes, pulls, and cuts into her nearly two-foot cube of clay. I try to keep everyone's attention on Yumi's work to interact with her sculpting, but some workshop members became deeply involved in their own playing, eyes closed. This was a new experience for both Yumi and CreW. After forty minutes Yumi puts down her tools and steps back from her sculpting table. Gradually CreW comes to a halt as well and a grateful silence ensues. Yumi's sculpture is quite detailed.

YUMI: The workshop's sounds were easy to sculpt from, and visual ideas came quite quickly.

EZRA: I just realized that I didn't play from Yumi's sculpting enough. I became trapped in my own playing. Can we try that again?

JON: Ezra, Sten Höstfält is coming for our second hour, but your observation is a good one. It takes time and practice to interact with another medium while doing your own work.

YUMI: May I leave the sculpture here to dry? I will have Yuto bring it home for me in a few days.

JON: Yumi, thank you again for coming today. Hajimemashite.

YUMI: Nice to meet you too, Jon.

EZRA: Wow, she is a good sculptor. Look at all those cool ears and mouths she made.

JON: Yes, the sculpture is worth a close look. For now, let's take a brief break until Sten Höstfält arrives.

> As I watched Yumi work, it became obvious that the sense of touch is very important to a sculptor. I could also see that Yumi was reacting closely to CreW's "music." The workshop had a tough time maintaining a focus on Yumi's sculpting since it's not every day a musician can "jam" with an artist from another medium. Yumi said that viewing sculpture is actually a performance art. An observer should walk around a sculpture to fully appreciate it. This walk is a type of dance.
>
> Fellow artists, try to arrange some live cross-medium happenings. I knew a painter, Ruth Brown, who would invite a music ensemble and a dance ensemble to improvise as she painted in her Cambridge home. I also have fond memories of working with Jack Powers's Cambridge-based Stone Soup Poets back in the 1970s.

OUR NEXT GUEST OF THE DAY: STEN HÖSTFÄLT

JON: I'm very excited to introduce you to Sten Höstfält, a Creative Workshop ancestor. It was about ten years ago that Sten graced CreW with his creative efforts. I actually remember one of Sten's pieces that incorporated consuming pieces of fruit. Sten is a leading innovative guitarist and composer working in the New York music scene today. He performs with some of the most original and unique voices in modern music. Sten has been called "highly exceptional" by legendary American music icon Jimmy Giuffre, and "virtuosic" by musical innovator Joe Maneri.

Welcome, Mr. Sten Höstfält.

MICROTONALISM

STEN: Thank you, Jon, and hello, everyone. I'm thrilled to be back at the workshop. It's a pleasure to be here and share some of my work with microtonality.

YUTO: What is microtonality?

STEN: There are various definitions. For now, we can say that microtonality is a system of pitches that explores beyond the equal tempered twelve-tone system. In Western civilization the equal tempered system is used for almost all the music we encounter. In order to deal with intervals smaller than equal temperament's semitone, I work with a system of seventy-two notes per octave that I learned from composer Joe Maneri at the New England Conservatory of Music. Maneri is continuing a tradition established by twentieth-century microtonal pioneers Julián Carillo, Alois Hába, and Ivan Wyschnegradsky. While a student here at Berklee, before studying microtonality, I had experimented with the parameters of pitch with Jon.

> To put microtonalism in perspective, a standard piano is tuned to the equal tempered system, having twelve notes in an octave. A seventy-two notes per octave microtonal piano keyboard would have to be six times the size of the standard piano. That would require an awfully big living room! *Genesis of a Music*, a book by the composer Harry Partch, has wonderful illustrations of instruments that he created for microtonal music performance.

TIM: Why seventy-two notes?

STEN: How many notes are there?

CreW blankly stares back at Sten, who turns and scratches on the board.

$$5,385$$

TIM: How did you come up with that number?

STEN: I just made it up to show you that there is really no actual number, and that the number of possible pitches is infinite. In the beginning was sound. Then man divided that into "equalized" entities. Now most of us are so used to the equal tempered system that we never question or go outside of the system. The notes we can actually hear within an octave, for the average person, is surely more than twelve. For generations we have been conditioned to hear the twelve-note system, and our ears tend to bring any *other* pitch to the closest pitch within the system. One method of approaching microtonality is to divide those twelve notes into smaller parts, which will help acquaint us with a greater pitch spectrum than we deal with on a daily basis. For me, using the standard tempered twelve-tone system as a base for departure makes navigation with microtonality easier than to abandon the twelve-tone system altogether.

TIM: Excuse me, Sten; seventy-two is a lot of notes. How do you keep track of all those notes?

BLUES FOR CREW"

STEN: I don't approach microtonality in a systematic manner. Rather, I try to cultivate my ears to hear the nature and characteristic sound of the microtones and the intervals and harmonies they imply. I feel that the best way to illustrate microtonality is to play it. I composed a piece called "blues for CreW" that will help us to get familiar with the quarter tone, twelfth tone, and sixth tone, and various combinations of those. Each voice of "blues for CreW" has a characteristic microtonal sound.

Fig. 11.1. "blues for CreW"

STEN: We will play through each individual voice, or part, together. We will start with dividing the semitone in half in order to hear the quarter tone that has the sound of a "semitone within the semitone." Bending a note a semitone up and finding the midpoint inside of that bend lets us find, hear, and control the quarter tone. Two of "blues for CreW's" five parts are written in quarter tones and are created to acclimate our ears to this interval. Then we will play and experience the twelfth tone, which at first may be described as a nuance, slightly higher or lower than standard pitch. We still use the regular, normally fretted pitches to help us navigate and for general fast, easy reference. The higher twelfth tone is easier to play and control than the lower twelfth tone on a regular fretted instrument, since we raise the pitch slightly by pressing it down just a little harder than normally. The sixth tone is an interval between the quarter tone and the twelfth tone, and is practically applied through a slight bend. Another part of "blues for CreW" is composed exclusively using sixth tones. Finally, the fifth part of the piece is a line that mixes quarter, sixth, and twelfth tones. Let's play each line together, in unison, to help familiarize us with each of these tones. As we proceed, gradually our ears will get accustomed to and recognize these tones. Once everyone is informed of the nature and sound of each part, CreW members will be assigned their parts. Then we can play and hear all the voices together.

The workshop practices Sten's "blues for CreW" and does a pretty good job of it!

JON: Sten, thank you for some great ideas, and really ear-opening stuff! I just love the new harmonic possibilities microtonality opens up, and "blues for CreW" gave us a perfect example.

STEN: I really appreciate your attention today. I enjoyed my visit.

CreW enthusiastically thanks Sten for his presentation.

JON: I hope you can stay for some of Roberto's homemade lemon pie.

STEN: That should be very easy for me to do.

> In music the traditional equal tempered system dictates certain pitches, or notes, as "correct." Imagine if an artist was restricted to only certain colors, a writer to only certain words, a dancer to only certain postures. Actually, these limitations may inspire possibilities that total freedom would not. Microtonalism, with its multitude of possible pitches, does not make it a more creative tool. Remember, it's not how much we've got that's important, it's how well we use what we've got.
>
> Try producing a work in your medium by limiting choices for yourself. Some infinite possibilities just may arise from the seeming limitations.

Our Surprise Guest: The Rubbertellie

JON: Some of you expressed an interest in the Rubbertellie, so I have brought it in as a surprise guest today. His nickname is RT. Having played the standard guitar for many years as an improviser, I invented the Rubbertellie to explore another instrumental medium. It's a standard guitar, with absolutely no additives, but approached in a totally nonstandard way. It is held and played differently, and tuned *quite* differently. The conceptual prefix "rubber" indicates that it has stretched the traditional boundaries of the guitar. It really is a polarity of the standard guitar. The suffix "tellie" is a shortening of Telecaster, a model of the Fender guitar company.

EZRA: Jon, how did you tune Rubbertellie when you played your "Doreen and Alice" track on *Dedications: Faces and Places*?

JON: On "Doreen and Alice" I tuned the Rubbertellie not by pitch but by a particular string tension feeling. The other Rubbertellie piece on the CD is called "Brother Sharpe," and it calls for a traditional equal tempered tuning. The bright, shimmering sound comes from placing a metal rod between the strings and the fingerboard. The "Brother Sharpe" theme is a quodlibet of "Frère Jacques," but in minor. The song is dedicated to an old friend, D. Sharpe, a longtime drummer with pianist and composer Carla Bley.

EZRA: That piece is pretty, and intense at the same time.

JON: Thank you, Ezra. There is a YouTube video of a lecture I gave about Rubbertellie at Bishop's College School in Quebec, which includes a rendition of "Brother Sharpe" (https://www.youtube.com/watch?v=tm57tCkhwbg).

MOMMY, WHAT'S A RUBBERTELLIE?

JON: I wrote a series of poems that are possible answers to the above often-asked question. Next to seeing and hearing the instrument, these poems are, I feel, the best answers. Or maybe better. In performance I recite the poems while reacting to them with the Rubbertellie. Here's one of the poems, in the form of a personals ad.

Not young, but gifted, and black, serial #28829, Fender, solid as they come, and been through lots. And more to come. Open to anything, and then some. A scrapper, a tapper, a regular Jekyll and Mr. Hyde. Likes hiking, and cooking, and acting, a real ham. Likable. Call 1-800-RUBBER. Nights only.

Readers, please note that the front and back cover photos of *Fresh Music* show Rubbertellie in action in Australia, performing "Rubbertellie Murals." See the copyright page of *Fresh Music*.

EZRA: Thanks for bringing in Rubbertellie, Jon.

JON: No problem, Ezra. RT loves the attention. I again thank Sten Höstfält for visiting us. And right now, let's eat some of that pie!

SEVERAL DAYS LATER . . .

When I was back in my studio, I looked more closely at the sculpture our guest Yumi produced, and studied the motif of mouths and ears throughout the piece. The mouths were opened wide as if they were screaming, and the ears had droplets of water flowing from them. I called Yumi to again thank her for coming to visit the workshop, and mentioned how impressed the workshop was with her work. I also asked her about her choice of motifs in her work. She simply responded that the workshop's creative enthusiasm was musically painful to her, which she expressed by sculpting crying ears and mouths screaming in pain!!

I didn't have the heart to tell the workshop.

CHAPTER 12 – WEEK 12
TASTE, SMELL, AND TOUCH FORMS, AND RECORDING SESSION

To draw, you must close your eyes, and sing. —Pablo Picasso

GUEST FEEDBACK

JON: Good morning, everyone. Before we begin our session today, how did you enjoy our guest artists last week?

MASTY: Yumi's visit was enlightening. Thank you, Yuto, for bringing Yumi to CreW.

YUTO: It was my pleasure, and she told me she really learned a lot from the experience. May I say that I was very impressed by Mr. Höstfält's discussion about microtones. It reminded me of a few weeks ago when Jon challenged me to transcribe his speaking voice. If my ears understood microtones better, perhaps I would have been able to do it. Spoken language is all about microtones!

JON: Yes, Yuto. In fact, I like to sometimes joke that J. S. Bach ripped us all off with his *Well-Tempered Clavier* opus, which some folks feel was a marketing ploy to sell everyone on the new equal tempered tuning system. "ONLY 12 NOTES! WHAT A RIP-OFF!!"

Able to modulate to any key with ease and perfectly in tune!! (well sorta)

As Sten mentioned, some microtonalists use a seventy-two-note chromatic scale—sixty more notes to work with than the twelve-note system, and in just one octave.

FUN WORKING WITH MICROTONES

JON: Check this out! Tim, please take up your guitar for a moment and tune your high E string down, an equally tempered half step, to E-flat. Check the tuning with your E-flat on the B string. Now I would like you to count how many *different* notes we can hear within that half step, between E-flat and E. First play your open E-flat string along with the fingered E-natural on your B string, a nice, rich, dissonant minor second. Continue playing the two strings as your nonfingering hand turns your high E-flat string's tuning peg up until you hear a change. Now do that again. Good, that's two turns, two discernible notes so far. Continue in this manner until your high E-flat becomes E-natural, in tune with the E on your B string. Okay, we have two turns already. Tim, continue turning.

The rest of the workshop counts.

"3! 4! 5! 6! 7! 8! 9! 10! 11! 12! 13! 14! 15! 16! 17! 18! 19! 20! 21!"

TIM: There it is Jon, back up to E-natural.

JON: Twenty-one turns; twenty-one notes we found existing between E-flat and E! Now, in one octave, we have found that there are at least 252 notes. That piano would need to be twelve times as large as a standard piano! The use of a twelve-note system may actually be a pragmatic choice. Twelve notes to an octave is enough to keep us busy for a while. I just think the possibilities are also exciting with the microtonal concept!

> Give a listen to the work of some microtonal composers. The String Quartet no. 2 of Alois Hába is a good place to start. Ivan Wyschnegradsky's Préludes for Piano are beautiful. I feel like I am entering another world when listening to these pieces. Can you think of some analogies to microtonalism in the work of visual artists? Perhaps a listen to Hába's and Wyschnegradsky's music will microtonally inspire you in your medium. Think of a painting in which minute variations of a color are used. The artist Frank Stella, a minimalist, comes to mind.

EZRA: What about your Rubbertellie? You work with microtones when you play it.

JON: Yes, on certain pieces I do, but I don't have full pitch control; there are just too many possible notes. My note choices are made more by ear, string tension, and touch on those pieces that are more "freely" tuned. Speaking of touch, now let's see how your senses of taste, touch, and smell have inspired you.

Taste, Smell, and Touch Forms

EZRA: Why did you wait until now, more than two months into the semester, to introduce the taste, touch, and smell theme?

JON: A good question. I wanted to wait until we started recording, since themes such as taste, smell, and touch pieces and next week's aleatoric pieces seem to work better in the moment, not premeditated or practiced.

"SUPER LEMON"

JON: Yuto, you have an idea to share?

YUTO: Yes, I do. As soon as you mentioned our assignment last week, I had an idea right away! In Japan we have some nice sweet treats. One of my favorites is a candy called Super Lemon. I brought some in today. I would like each of us to play a solo improvisation inspired by the taste of Super Lemon. I wish we could film ourselves also because the facial reactions to the tasting would be hilarious.

Bruno offers his camera to me to film the Super Lemon–tasting players for Yuto.

JON: Yuto, we could begin our first recording session with a video. A quick sound check and we should be on our way. Please direct the workshop, Yuto.

YUTO: Thank you, Jon. Make sure we capture the sound of us unwrapping the candy. We will use canon technique. Wait about five seconds after your neighbor opens, tastes, and begins playing their Super Lemon, before opening yours. Let's begin with Roberto. We can really only do one take of this piece.

Yuto was right about the facial expressions; having a video is important here. The Super Lemon candy lasts for about ten minutes.

JON: Nice candy, Yuto! It comes on strong, mellows out, and then comes on strong again. Almost like it's time-release candy!

YUTO: I am happy you enjoyed it. Another of my favorite candies is Unagi Pie, which is named after one of my favorite foods, eel.

CHESTER: I think I'll pass on that one.

YUTO: Chester, Unagi Pie is actually a very sweet pastry-type snack, there is no eel in it.

ROBERTO: I can see why recording the *first* playing of Super Lemon makes sense. A second playing of Super Lemon would lose the vitality of the conception. I should try some in my Lemon Pie recipe.

JON: Roberto, your pies were delicious. To continue the taste segment of today's session, here is a multimedia taste piece composed by Daniel, a CreW ancestor from several years ago, and a culinary artist like yourself, Roberto.

> Dancers, painters, writers, actually, all of you, pop a Super Lemon, and in real time represent your reactions through your medium. Any confectionary shop will have its own version of Super Lemon. Super Lemon is not cheap stuff. There's a YouTube video of babies' facial reactions to their first tastes of lemon. Very cute.

DANIEL'S "BLUESSHAPE RICE PIECE"

JON: Daniel had the workshop use their taste to inspire their writing, which inspired their drawing with pastels, which inspired their playing!

EZRA: Sounds like a Rube Goldberg creation.

JON: Right, Ezra.

YUTO: Who is Rube Goldberg?

JON: Rube Goldberg was a cartoonist, and I bet that Tim, scientist that he is, could explain better than I what a Rube Goldberg is.

TIM: Actually, I once entered a Rube Goldberg competition in which we had to come up with the most outlandish machine to do a very simple job.

YUTO: I know what a Rube Goldberg is now. These are very popular in Japan.

JON: Here are the details of Daniel's piece. He uses some BluesShape thinking here.

Daniel's BluesShape Rice Piece
Section One: The Tasting
Each player is given three samples of rice dishes to taste:
a I chord rice dish, a IV chord rice dish, and a V chord rice dish.
Players taste the I chord rice dish and write a description
of their tasting experience.
Players taste the IV chord rice dish and write a description
of their tasting experience.
Players taste the V chord rice dish and write a description
of their tasting experience.

Section Two: The Drawing
Players are then given pastels and paper for drawing. The piece of paper is divided into a
blank I section, a blank IV section, and a blank V section.
Together the players begin to read aloud their written descriptions from their rice tasting
and, at the same time, interpret what they are reading with the pastels and paper.
First the I chord rice dish is read and drawing is done, then the IV chord rice dish, and
finally the V chord rice dish.

Section Three: The Sound Interpretation
The players now take their instruments and improvise from their three drawings,
in BluesShape order. These can be done as a group or as solo statements.
FINE

CreW seemed impressed.

"Wow, I'd like to hear that!"

"And see it."

"And taste it. That made me hungry."

CHESTER: Actually, it sounds like Daniel was catching up on homework. He included several themes all rolled into one there.

JON: Chester, you may have something there.

Daniel's rice piece form would make a nice scenario for a cross-medium jam with some artist friends. Try three different candy flavors instead of rice. Of course the V chord would have to be Super Lemon. Or maybe Red Hots! In section three you can scat or whistle a reaction to the pastel drawings.

EZRA'S "JELLY BEAN STUDY"

EZRA: I have another taste piece if that's all right?

JON: The more the merrier, Ezra.

EZRA: In the Mall in Boston's Prudential Center there's a jelly bean shop, and they have hundreds of flavors of jelly beans, some of them quite gross! So I thought of a cool concert piece. Have CreW improvise while eating a particular flavor of jelly bean while the audience, at the same time, is eating the *same* flavor jelly bean. Audience participation.

JON: Ezra, I am also a big fan of getting the audience creatively involved in a performance beyond the listening level. I call it "audience precipitation." Get 'em working and sweating!

EZRA: Can we try my "Jelly Bean Study" with CreW next week? I will bring in eight flavors of beans, one for each of us. Eat your own bean, and improvise a solo while the rest of CreW is eating the same flavor.

JON: Sure. Between Roberto's lemon pies, Yuto's Super Lemons, and Ezra's jelly beans, we are all going to need a diet soon!

EZRA: And a good dentist.

MASTY'S "FLOWERS"

JON: I've been meaning to ask, Masty. For whom is that lovely bouquet of flowers intended?

MASTY: They are for everyone, and they are for a smell piece for today. I collected them by the Muddy River in the Fens. There are so many different flowers in bloom right now. Each workshop member has their own special flower. Smell your flower, and at the same time, play the smelling experience. Several seconds should do it.

JON: A really nice moment piece, Masty.

Masty passes out flowers and we record some brief smell-inspired solos. Part of Roberto's solo consists of a really cool loud sneeze.

ROBERTO: I'm sorry, Masty. I have a sensitive nose, and have allergic reactions sometimes.

MASTY: That's fine, Roberto. The sneeze worked perfectly.

> Your artistic thoughts about and your medium reactions to these taste and smell pieces may look somewhat nonrepresentational. Describing a particular taste or smell with words is fairly impossible. In fact, your nonrepresentational visual interpretation probably does a better job.

MEMORIES OF TYLER

JON: Here is a powerful sense of smell story. I had a student, Tyler, who was diagnosed with multiple sclerosis. I watched Tyler over a period of seventeen years slowly succumb to this disease. In his last years of life Tyler was blind, bedridden, and in a constant fetal position, barely able to talk or move. On one of my final visits to him I asked if he would like to go outside. He slightly nodded yes. We rented a specially designed wheelchair and took Tyler for a stroll. I thought to use his still active sense of smell as an avenue for him to enjoy the outdoors. I grabbed bits of pine needles, leaves, and flowers, holding them near his nose. I could tell he was enjoying the smells by his familiar wide smile. He was the bravest person I have ever met.

"FUR MUSIC"

JON: I have seen only one piece of music that called upon the sense of touch, "Fur Music." The piece consisted of five different strips of fur. The player was directed to feel each strip and improvise musically from the sensations. I realize that during our playing, as musicians, touch is possibly the most important sense after our sense of hearing. Applying articulation with lips and fingers is all about tactile sensuality. I once performed at an institute for the deaf, and the audience danced to the music's vibration. Touch.

THE INFINITY OF LIMITATIONS

Last week I suggested trying to do a work in which you impose a limit on yourself. Work with only three colors, three shapes, or three dance postures. Here is a piece in which I limit CreW members to one small area of their guitar fingerboard. It's amazing to hear the variety of ways workshop members play within these particular parameters.

"SHAMISEN SAM"

JON: Here is a variation of "Shamisen Sam," a concept piece that I would like to try with our guitarists as part of our recording session today. I would like each of you to perform a solo for exactly three minutes.

Anything goes, but with some parameters imposed—limitations you might say. I would like each of you to use only your top three strings: your open high E string, B string, and G string, and the following fingered notes. Here it is on the board.

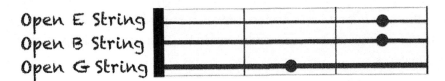

Fig. 12.1. "Shamisen Sam"

MASTY: That's just a G major pentatonic scale.

JON: Right, Masty. But you have to bring it to life, in any manner you wish. Use it to play a melody, chords, harmonics, use any rhythms and articulations, and, of course, use comprovisational integrity. So I would like each of you to record an exactly three-minute improvisation, by yourself, with no one else in the room. Later I will bring the tracks together as one piece with a common thread, your initial limitations. Yuto, you go first. Everyone else, let's step outside. Press this button when you're ready to play, then at exactly three minutes, stop the recording with the space bar. Then Masty, it's your turn.

The workshop gradually completes their solos for "Shamisen Sam."

MASTY: I felt that the limitations, only being able to use a small section of the instrument, opened up possibilities for me that total freedom would not.

JON: Good, Masty; and the guitar is a great instrument for finding these limitations.

MASTY: Who is Shamisen Sam, Jon?

JON: A shamisen is a Japanese plucked string instrument. It has three gut strings and a rectangular-shaped body that is wrapped with the skin of a snake, a deadly pit viper called a Habu. I don't know who Sam is.

HEAVY RUBBER

JON: Earlier in the semester I mentioned "Happy Birthday Rubbertellie," a piece that is all about limitations and audience participation. It's part of *Heavy Rubber,* the documentary film about Rubbertellie.

EZRA: Can we watch it together?

JON: To work with your different schedules, I will show it in the hour before and the hour after next week's session, if anyone is interested.

AND THEN I BROKE IT TO THEM

I told the workshop that during Yumi's visit she had a rather powerful experience sculpting with us. I mentioned that if you can make someone *strongly* react to your work, as Yumi obviously reacted, this is as important as having someone simply love your work—perhaps even more important; creating a stirring of possibilities in the observer, and helping them realize that infinity still exists.

In fact, Yumi mentioned that she would never have considered the ears and mouth motifs in her work if it wasn't for the horribly brilliant creative work of CreW.

We'll do some more recording next week.

Chapter 13 – Week 13
A Free Jam and Some Chance Music for Good Luck

Chance favors the prepared mind. —Louis Pasteur

Heavy Rubber

TIM: Thanks for showing us the *Heavy Rubber* film, Jon. It was worth coming in early for.

JON: Thank you, Tim.

BRUNO: Please don't say any more about the film. I'm staying for the second showing after today's session.

JON: Okay everyone, let's record Masty's "Dominoes Study #1," her game-inspired piece. Grab your folders.

> Readers, you will find Masty's entire "Dominoes Study #1" back in your folder, chapter 15. Even if you are not a music reader, follow along with Masty's dialogue as she describes the gravity and magnetism at work in her piece.

Masty's "Dominoes Study #1"

JON: Masty, can you discuss your game concept here?

MASTY: As children, back home, we loved to watch our father and uncles playing the game of dominoes. When they finished their games we would sneak off with the domino sets—not to play the game, but to carefully set up the dominoes in a cool pattern. Then *push . . .* we'd watch the pattern of tiles gracefully collapsing to the floor. Endlessly we would create patterns, choose who got to be the pusher, and then . . . Years later, a counterpoint teacher used this same domino activity as an analogy to illustrate intervals resolving tendencies downward and upward. I thought, Why not imagine myself pushing the intervals, tapping into their tilelike gravitational and magnetic energies? Hence, this woodwind quartet.

A hand shoots up. "Can you give us a brief analysis?"

MASTY: Intervals have basic gravitational and magnetic resolution tendencies; fourths have a tendency to move to thirds, sevenths to sixths, and seconds to thirds, to point out a few. I have these interval dynamics taking place, but to increase intensity I let the unresolved note remain *along with* the resolved note, to create a pleasing ambiguity. Here is part of the piece.

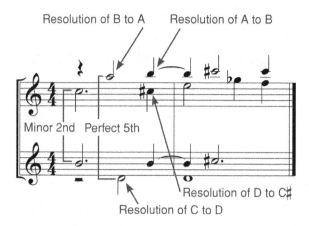

Fig. 13.1. Masty's "Dominoes Study #1" Example

MASTY: The opening two notes B and C are a minor second interval apart. I have the B resolve to the note A, now in the top voice, creating a traditional resolution to the interval of a third. I let the B note in the third voice continue to sustain, creating a nice, rich harmonic quality. The D entering in the bottom voice is the resolution of the C. Now a perfect fifth interval appears between the D and the A. I follow this interval plan generally throughout. Let's record it please.

In my "Dominoes Study #1" musical gravity is in a sense being denied, having both a resolved and unresolved note at the same time. I think of the perspective I have seen in some cubist paintings and sculpture where the background and foreground are in the same plane.

A SQUABBLE AND CREW'S "FREE JAM"

JON: That is a really nice study, Masty.

CHESTER: I agree. But at this point, between all of Masty's technical mumbo jumbo and all that sight-reading, I . . .

JON: Pardon me, Chester??!!

CHESTER: Apologies, Masty, for me it is . . .

JON: Well, it wouldn't be if you would just study! Through my own study of intervals they have become second nature and now open up some really nice possibilities for my composing and improvising! And this reading was easy. Why, any . . .

CHESTER: Masty, I didn't mean to insult you. Jon, could we play a free jam for a change?

JON: Sure. Let's channel all this energy into something constructive.

CreW, let's record this jam, no parameters set initially. Just stop when you feel that you have completed your free piece.

CreW begins playing, really gets into the improvisation, and comes to a conclusion after about twenty minutes.

JON: That was pretty impressive, and your playing sounds like you have really learned to communicate this semester, to work as a team. A crew! And this teamwork, this sharing, helped you build an impressive, developed piece, from no initial plan. I'm happy we have that on the recording.

YUTO: I remember trying to jam freely with friends, and we would always end up in the same place. I now feel that I have many more possible paths to take thanks to my colleagues.

JON: Thanks, Yuto. CreW, your communication ability as performers, composers, and leaders has to be practiced regularly. Use it or lose it! After the semester is over, be sure to keep this flame alive for the rest of your lives. Next week I'm going to share some letters that I have received in which your CreW ancestors share how they are keeping their Creative Workshop flame alive.

CHESTER: I'm sorry Masty; I was being foolish before.

MASTY: That's fine, Chester. Somebody has to be.

Chance Music

JON: Since this is our thirteenth week of workshop, I thought that for good luck we could try some aleatoric ideas. In fact, Chester, this is a totally nontechnical technique. Decisions are made by chance with a deck of cards, the roll of the dice, or by choosing straws, for example.

BRUNO: Do you mean like gambling?

JON: Well, we're not going to be losing any money here. Essentially, we're letting something other than our sometimes tired creative mind make decisions for us, like spinning a bottle, as we tried a few weeks ago. The tossing of a coin to decide up or down. We could cut a deck of cards to decide an interval, or check the daily lottery number to inspire a melodic theme. If it's good enough for Mozart, it's good enough for us.

> Besides Mozart, some aleatoricists include choreographer Merce Cunningham, artist Robert Rauschenberg, and composer John Cage. Some feel that the seeming randomness of Jackson Pollock's painting technique, hurling or dripping paint onto the canvas, was aleatoric. I disagree, and feel that Pollock was in full command with his technique. It's interesting to ponder the point at which material is derived randomly or planned. I know that when I do sketching it sure seems hit or miss. An organization by the name of MAMA, the Movement of Aleatoric Modern Artists, has an interesting website, aleatoricart.com.

"THE FIRST TEN ROLLS OF THE DICE" PIECE

JON: While shopping last Christmas holiday, I stopped at a really cool games and hobby shop. A display of colorful dice attracted me. In the case were standard six-sided dice, along with four-sided and up to 100-sided dice—yes, a 100-sided die. I decided to build an aleatoric composition using dice as my decision maker. I bought a pretty blue twelve-sided die to make pitch or note decisions for me, a green ten-sided die to make rhythmic decisions, a yellow eight-sided die for dynamic decisions, and a bright red four sided, pyramid-shaped die to help make register decisions—the octave to place the note in.

Fig. 13.2. The Dice

Over a period of about two months I would occasionally ask folks to roll the four dice. Then I would enter the results into a computer spreadsheet program. I never rolled the dice myself; I wanted to totally distance myself to make the work as aleatorically pure as possible.

I rolled along until I realized that the one decision I still needed to make was when to stop bothering people and end the piece! That actually became an easy decision, and an aleatoric one. One day, by chance, I lost all my dice! I figured that was as good an aleatoric cue to end the piece as any.

So here are the first ten rolls of the dice, brought to manuscript paper and in proportional notation. I'll draw them on the board.

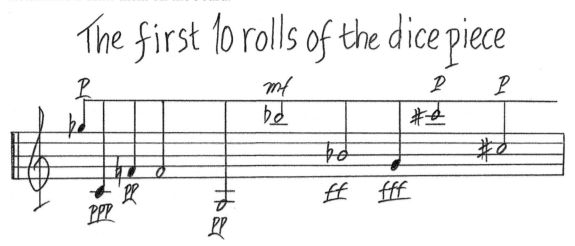

Fig. 13.3. "The First Ten Rolls of the Dice" Piece

For this piece, the only two decisions that *I made* was to play it on solo guitar and to use dice as a decision tool. Do I like the piece? Of course. It's my aleatoric baby! In this piece I am using aleatoric decision making in a fairly traditional way. In a composition you may consider a decision by a performer as an aleatoric element. The possibilities and choices are endless, and probably sitting in your pocket right now!

TIM: In a sense isn't life *all* chance-operated?

JON: That's for you to determine, Tim.

A Glance at Next Week

JON: Next week is our last week of school, and there is no particular assignment. I will be discussing some international CreW workshops that I have done.

Quotes from Notable Folks

Readers and fellow artists, I enjoyed the squabble between Masty and Chester about the importance of theoretical thinking in the arts. Here are some quotes that give a glimpse at the idea that there are as many ways to create art as there are artists!

Does creation reside in the idea or in the action?   —Alan Bowness

Imagination is more important than knowledge.   —Albert Einstein

There are two ways of constructing a work of art. One is by making decisions at each step, another by inventing a system to make decisions.
—Sol LeWitt

I start a canvas without a thought of what it might eventually become.
—Joán Miró

I paint objects as I think them not as I see them.   —Pablo Picasso

I think of my pictures as dramas. Neither the action, nor the actors can be anticipated, or described in advance. They begin as an unknown adventure in an unknown space.   —Mark Rothko

CHAPTER 14 – WEEK 14
CreW on the Road

I can't understand why people are frightened of new ideas. I'm frightened of the old ones. —John Cage

This chapter shows how CreW philosophy and techniques can work in various group situations. Teaching is a sacred, ancient performance art, and conducting a workshop in your medium can be a great learning experience. It's exciting to have a group of people as your medium—to move your ideas through, observing the reactions, and creating feedback.

JON: Good morning, and welcome to our last workshop meeting of the semester. It has been a really nice semester, thanks to your wonderful creative energy. Take the Creative Workshop spirit with you and let it inspire all your endeavors; use workshop techniques every day as a performer, composer, artist, and as a teacher. I would like to share some of my own personal experiences using workshop techniques in various settings. I will also share with you some letters from your Creative Workshop ancestors.

First, let's go to Italy.

A "CORONATION" AND "DEMOCRATIC CHORALE": ITALIAN STYLE

Here is an article I wrote for the Berklee magazine *Berklee Today* that documents the Creative Workshop Ensemble in action, as well as showing inspiration derived from the wonderful Italian food!

LA DANZA DELLA SCARPETTA: A PERUGIAN RECIPE

The Italian word *scarpetta* translates literally into "little shoe." Gastronomically speaking, *scarpetta* refers to the art of gracefully skating a bit of finely crusted bread around a plate to absorb the delicious finale of a wonderful meal. I was first introduced to the art of scarpetta at Ristorante La Rosetta in Perugia, Italy, an ancient city perched on a hill in the Umbria region. For several years I have performed and conducted Berklee-sponsored workshops there as part of the Umbria Jazz Festival. When invited to participate in this year's twenty-fifth anniversary of the Berklee in Umbria program, I responded, "It would be my pasta—I mean my pleasure—to go!"

Other than eating and drinking well, my main function during the festival is to direct master classes and prepare student ensembles for a concert experience: four ensembles in just four rehearsals. The daily balance, the cycle, and the symbiotic relationship between the intensity of working with the ensembles at the school down the hill from the city center and the return trip to Ristorante La Rosetta for nourishment provide an important combination: a recipe that fuels the creative spirit.

DRAWING ON THE SENSES

When preparing the ensembles for the concert I drew on communication techniques from the Creative Workshop, a performance class I have developed and directed at Berklee for more than thirty years. The fundamental philosophy of the workshop is to draw inspiration from anything in the universe, from alphabets to zodiacs. In Perugia, that might be a plate of Trenette al Pesto (a heavenly nest of pasta with a basil sauce scented with a fragrance that rings of sun-speckled fields of green). Each ensemble workshop has a unique set of ingredients: players with a range of abilities and instruments. I relish the challenge of creating a special musical recipe with the ingredients at hand. How about eleven guitars?

On the opening day of the workshops, I waited for the arrival of my first ensemble. A trumpet player walked in, followed by a guitarist, a drummer, two pianists, another guitarist, a bassist, and then, to my surprise, a harpist slowly and carefully wheeling in a lovely golden-colored harp. Following her were another guitarist, a saxophonist, and two drummers. The players were very interesting ingredients. "Please introduce yourselves," I said. "Isabella," the harpist responded. "Queen Isabella!" I thought excitedly, and realized that with a harpist named Isabella in a magical setting like Perugia, with its castlelike walls, cobbled paths and steps, sculptured archways, and bells tolling, we should try "The Coronation," one of my creative workshop pieces that uses story form. The approach is for musicians to portray the various characters of a story: in this case, the crowning of a king and queen. Isabella is the queen, Stefano (one of the pianists) is the king, and the other instrumentalists play the roles of villagers and singers: the creators of a medieval ambience, a perfect setting for a coronation.

Later, during one of my many repasts at Ristorante La Rosetta, as I finished the final fragrant morsels of a plate of Trenette al Pesto, I envisioned a new piece. As I watched my hand skate circles with a bit of bread around the plate, I imagined a scarpetta-inspired dance with a calypso-flavored melody and harmony. After my last swipe of bread, I ran excitedly—but slowly— to my room to sketch "La Danza della Scarpetta" for my afternoon ensemble.

"La Danza della Scarpetta" is a simple dance; it's as easy to perform as eating a bowl of pasta, and incorporates some age-old Italian hand gestures. You simply stand and imagine a plate in front of your nose. Take your right hand and bring your thumb, index, and middle fingertips together as though you're holding an imaginary bit of bread. While singing the lyric *scarpetta* (see the musical example above), move the hand clockwise around the edge of the plate. For the repetition of the word *scarpetta*, make a counter-clockwise circle with your left hand. For the lyrics "Mmm! Mmm!," simply point your right index finger lightly into your right cheek and make a couple of little twists. Then do the same with your left index finger and left cheek, for the next "Mmm! Mmm!" (see the example above).

Ensemble members danced and played excitedly, and during the concert their performance inspired the audience to sing and dance. "La Danza della Scarpetta" was a hit.

My student ensembles' performances were filled with a youthful drive and exuberance that rivaled the energy emanating from the main stage at this year's Umbria Jazz Festival. The joy of working with the students and sharing their excitement during the concert is hard to describe—as difficult, let's say, as describing the delights of Fritto di Mozzarella (a dish of lightly battered and fried buffalo mozzarella), or Tagliatta di Petto di Pollo con Arugula e Pomodorini (a grilled-chicken dish).

Some readers may wonder what I did with the ensemble that had eleven guitar players. Actually, some of the sweetest music of my four concert ensembles came from the two guitar orchestras that consisted essentially of beginner-level guitarists with little or no experience. A unique ensemble can produce some unique music.

For a guitar orchestra piece, I again drew on La Rosetta's menu for inspiration, including Lasagna Tartufo (a lovely ensemble of layers of homemade pasta, local cheeses, truffles, and cream sauce) and Insalata Pescatora (a rich assemblage of seafood: calamari, shrimp, mussels, and octopus). For one guitar ensemble, instead of "homogenizing" the players to conform to one idea, I decided to create layers: that is, a musical lasagna of sorts. I had the guitarists display their own particular personality—their own flavor, if you will—by creating a brief musical idea and playing it repeatedly, solidly, and with confidence. We played the spicy mix of layers, added group vocalizations in a common key and tempo, and titled the piece "African Village." The final performance went so well that audience members remarked that the "composition" reminded them of the music of Steve Reich, King Crimson, and Igor Stravinsky. And that was with early-level musicians playing!

As you can see, the symbiotic relationship of food, environment, and music is a real thing for me. I hear the food, smell the cobblestones, and taste the music. In the Creative Workshop philosophy, we think of ourselves as "polyartists": that is, artists in all media. We experience all media through all expressions and senses such as hearing a painting, singing a flower, dancing to a recipe. I employ this holistic approach in my new book, *Fresh Music: Explorations with the Creative Workshop Ensemble for All Musicians, Artists, and Teachers*, and invite musicians, artists, and teachers of all persuasions to participate. In the Creative Workshop Ensemble, simple, organic concepts and language translate easily to various artistic media. As polyartists, and as Homo sapiens, we share a common, mutual medium, our being. Through our chosen artistic medium, we share our essential selves with others. For me, this sharing is the true beauty of the arts.

> Readers: You may wish to go to the YouTube video of "The Coronation" and watch and listen as I share the workshop experience with you. Here is the link: http://www.youtube.com/watch?v=RUtbbJyAYfE

> As you can see and hear in the YouTube video, this ensemble performed this totally improvised piece well. The only "concrete" preparation was in using "Democratic Chorale" technique for the ending of the piece and a *ritornello* (a return) to the opening chorale texture until the final conducted chord—of course, a democratically chosen one.

CREW AT THE WELLESLEY MIDDLE SCHOOL

The workshop began early, at 7:20 a.m., with a bedraggled group of thirty middle school students, the concert band, led by the ebullient Henry Platt, who had graciously invited me to the school to lead a workshop. I arrived with my instrument, a pile of papers and plastic, and a bag of gourmet jelly beans.

I began with an introduction to Creative Workshop philosophy that quickly moved into a fun round of communication studies. First Mime Study, with bodies only, with the entire thirty-member ensemble *silently* miming my sound-filled body antics; clapping, sneezing, etc. Hesitant at first, they eventually did very well. I picked up my instrument and had the band, in full force, with instruments held, respond mimelike and silently to my playing. Next, each student played a duet with me with our instruments sounding. I was amazed at the range of response ability. I would stay with a student, simplify my playing until they could hear themselves, hear me, and react to me. Things were going well. The more hesitant students were loosening up. Egos were melting quickly.

I also tried Sprecht-Blots with sections of the orchestra, beginning with the percussion section with the word "hail." First responses were feeble, muscle-memorized reactions. I coached them into really becoming HAIL!!! I tried more words. "Ping-pong" with trombones garnered a better reaction. "Ice skating" with flutes stimulated a very sweet reaction, conservative, until I suggested a more extended Sprecht-Blot, "Olympic-level skating with a triple-toe loop"!! A nice reaction to "sailboats" with the clarinets was followed by an incredibly intense response of dry, tortured sounds to "desert" with the trumpets. A great start for the workshop.

My most memorable moment at the Wellesley Middle School was the group's performance of "The Happy Birthday Concerto." Here is the concerto, for thirty-piece orchestra.

"THE HAPPY BIRTHDAY CONCERTO FOR MIDDLE SCHOOL ORCHESTRA VARIATIONS"

Before beginning "The Happy Birthday Concerto" I asked the Wellesley orchestra, "What is the most common song in the world?" After tossing around a few titles, we agreed on the birthday theme. Here below is the scenario of how we built the concerto together.

> The following "Happy Birthday" variations were created through a communal effort of the Wellesley concert band, of course prodded by me. Joint creative efforts and ideas are really the fruits of workshop consciousness.

Variation #1
I first had the ensemble *sing* the familiar happy birthday theme.

Variation #2
Then I had them *imagine* themselves playing the birthday theme with their instruments.

Variation #3

Next I asked the group to play the "Happy Birthday" theme starting on a concert F-natural until they were all playing the theme together "perfectly," which took about seven to eight times passing through the theme. Watching the searching eyes and ears of the students as they slowly found the theme was exciting.

Variation #4

I passed out the "Happy Birthday" music printed on clear plastic sheeting. We played the theme in original form, then discussed "Fireworks" technique, an extraction technique, and tried some possibilities. I introduced collage technique and tried some possibilities. Then I had students actually write a solo statement of their own on the manuscript paper provided. Some were very timid variations, and others more daring. Thanks to the clear plastic copies of the birthday theme I provided, we tried doing original retrograde, upside down, and upside down retrograde variations. Finally, we played all four variations together.

We used "Democratic Chorale" technique to choose a closing chord for the piece.

I gave jelly beans to the student with the closest birthday, and then gave the group an assignment: create a piece using the remaining jelly beans.

> One can continue with other possibilities. My point here with having the orchestra create and execute the above ideas is to help the students feel empowered, to truly reach deeply into their creative selves, which is something many ensemble situations can use. I would love to try this piece with the Boston Symphony Orchestra!

CreW on the Road at the Rimon School in Tel Aviv
"DOREEN AND ALICE" WITH 120 PERFORMERS!

I was invited to the Rimon School, a well-respected jazz academy in Tel Aviv, to perform and conduct workshops as part of the International Association of Jazz Educators conference. A magical Creative Workshop moment occurred here. Dave Liebman, the renowned saxophonist, asked me to do a lecture that tapped into some of CreW's techniques. The theme I chose was "Playing an Ancient Instrument: The Human Voice." As part of the lecture I had the audience perform "Doreen and Alice."

The entire audience of 120 people performed an incredible, magically beautiful rendition.

Stories from CreW Ancestors

The following statements from Creative Workshop Ensemble ancestors present a mixture of memories and illustrate how the workshop is still inspiring today.

Joe Cohn, Fall 1978, Member of the first Creative Workshop Ensemble

The Creative Workshop was the most important experience I had at Berklee. It was a real example of a musical setting that would open up for me understandings of how music can really be alive. It gave me the chance to be an integral part of the music, and feel equally responsible for the music as a whole. I learned about real music making as opposed to just learning basics.

While the basics are important, the workshop music opened the door to playing with depth. I look back at the times with the quartet as being the most revealing about how to play great music with no limitations. I wish I could have had many more years of that invaluable experience. I'm very proud to have been a member of the very first Creative Workshop.

Bill Frisell, Fall 1978, Member of the first Creative Workshop Ensemble

I moved to Boston in 1975 in search of something. Music. It was there I had the good fortune to meet and study with Jon Damian. I played in one of his early Creative Workshop Ensembles (a guitar quartet with Jon, Joe Cohn, Eric Jensen, and myself). Jon helped me to find many of the things I was looking for. He showed me new ways of looking at what I already knew . . . things that were right there in front of me . . . turning them around and seeing them from a different angle. New possibilities. He opened the window and the door. He gave me the keys . . . a rope to hang onto allowing larger leaps. To not be afraid of jumping off . . . to make mistakes . . . to learn. He came along just at the right moment. I'm so lucky (blessed) to know him. He continues to be an inspiration. Jon has spent his life dedicated to finding truth, beauty, and expanding the imagination.

Eric Jensen, 1978, Member of the first Creative Workshop Ensemble

I was fortunate to be part of Jon Damian's first Creative Workshop along with Jon, Joe Cohn, and Bill Frisell. Berklee had many wonderful guitar ensembles at the time, most modeled after the big band paradigm. Jon's concept was radically different. Each of us had unique musical personalities. Rather than play primarily soli passages, then individual solos, we were encouraged to express our individuality to the max. Many of the pieces contained conceptual directions and graphic notation. This opened my mind to new worlds that went way beyond post-bebop and chord scales. Never had I experienced such a rich tapestry of creative possibilities from four guitars. That experience was a turning point in the development of my musical personality. It was a blast!

Henry Platt, Fall 1980, Wellesley Middle School

My name is Henry Platt, and I teach Concert Bands, Jazz Bands, and general music at Wellesley Middle School outside of Boston. I studied guitar with Professor Damian in the early 1980s at Berklee College of Music. When Jon came out with his first book, *The Guitarist's Guide to Composing and Improvising*, I ran out and got a copy. I was intrigued by the description of the Creative Workshop in the book, and eventually decided to invite Professor Damian out to our school to teach the Creative Workshop with students in grades 6, 7 & 8. Creative Workshop with Professor Damian has now become an annual event. He has performed "The Coronation" and "Variations on Happy Birthday" with our Morning Jazz Band, and "Doreen and Alice" with Grade 6 music students.

As a result of these sessions, the students have become much more open to exploring new horizons in performance, and many have overcome their apprehension about standing up and improvising in front of the band. In our Grade 6 composition unit, students create and perform their own percussion ensembles. After experiencing the Creative Workshop with Jon, they were eager to explore and experiment on their own. The result was a group of wonderful performances with titles like "The Construction Site," "Bowling Alley," "Spring Rainstorm." Thanks to Jon's workshop, the students learned that they could use traditional percussion instruments in nontraditional ways, and even create their own instruments to produce new sounds. The workshop really transformed their thinking about music, sound, and creativity. The Creative Workshop concept has given me a broad palette to draw from in designing lessons for teaching everything from form to tone quality.

Sten Höstfält, Fall 1990

The Creative Workshop provided an outlet and forum to focus on personal creative ideas through collaborative sharing and processing, rather than results, ratings, credits, and purely personal achievement.

In the workshop we worked with everything from graphic notation to visual and performance art, to strictly notated polyphonic classical pieces. Thanks to Jon for being such a fantastic, subtle guide, and for so discreetly opening so many doors. His work and the workshop will live as long as there are participants willing to share their ideas and music.

Mastaneh Nazarian, Spring and Fall 1993

I remember the time after a concert when the workshop went out to South Boston for pizza. When reading the menu on the wall, done in those little white plastic letters, my brain was trying to put its contents into a "workshopian" order, since bits of the words were missing; anch vies, heese, g occi, you get the picture. This related to the type of exercise the group did with extraction development. If I have my brain tuned in to the Creative Workshop mode, everywhere I look can inspire a composition.

Phillip van Endert, Fall 1993

The environment of Berklee was very important to me, and helped me enormously to learn how to play my instrument and to deal with all the different facets that come along with music. But being every day in the situation to react to chord changes, scales, harmony, ear training, etc. could sometimes also turn into a quite scientific way to approach music. Because of that the Creative Workshop was always like an oasis to me. It opened all the other doors in my head that are important to directly feel and play music, and to react and talk to my fellow musicians through my instrument. It was quite a challenge to be in the workshop, but right from the first moment it was all about pure music, and every session evoked and brought back my true feelings about experiencing music. Today this open-minded approach is still with me as a performer and listener, and I hope that this will never change.

Chris Bartos, Fall 1996

Jon walks into the small fifth floor guitar department classroom, eyes beaming with enthusiasm as it is a new semester for the Creative Workshop, and there are five participants, just thirsting for knowledge.

An explanation for the conceptual piece "African Village" is given, and within minutes our world of standard notation, grip chords, and chord-scale monkey business is shattered, leaving us with the profound realization that music exists everywhere, and that by using stimuli other than traditional music language, one can easily be transported into an infinite world of new discoveries.

Inspired by these lessons, I purchase a dozen assorted donuts and challenge myself to use the textures and color of the doughy goodness to spawn solo, duo, and group improvisations with CreW.

This tackle box full of lessons and concepts absorbed during my Creative Workshop experience continues to greatly influence my life as a musician, producer, and multimedia artist. I am eternally grateful for the experience.

Francesco Guaiana, Spring 2001

The workshop was one of the best of my Berklee studies. I had a chance to finally approach music in a different way. Jon's intention was to take all of us beyond our capabilities and play in a way that we didn't know before. I remember when he made us compose from other forms of art, like poetry and film.

Stephane Wrembel, Fall 2001

I have such great memories from the Creative Workshop Ensemble I took with Jon Damian, perhaps the most creative guitar teacher in the world today. His strength is to see music in every aspect of life and nature, and to convey this fantastic vision to his students. His class makes me think of the creative classes my fellow actors talk about; not the class that allows you to recite Shakespeare or play the classical Greek authors, but the class that teaches you to be in contact with the deepest and most mysterious areas of your subconscious; to be creative, spontaneous, and in touch with your true self. Jon's approach is very unconventional and adventurous, modern and, at the same time, timeless. I remember scoring a spoon, a candle, a chess game, '80s computer cards, piling up melodies, playing harmonic puzzles, having so many laughs playing our national tongue twisters (we were six different nationalities!), and many, many other things. Jon would act like a coach, encouraging us to find new ways to invent within ourselves. Being a film composer and a concert artist specialized in live improvisation, I received the most valuable elements from Jon's teaching, opening a door of endless creativity in me.

Craig Ferguson, Spring 2003

When I think back on my times with the Creative Workshop, I think about the intense communication between the musicians in the room. Truly creative music cannot exist without listening, connecting, and reacting within a group. My experience in the Creative Workshop helped me learn how to better communicate with musicians and has been essential in my career as a working professional musician.

Andres Ponciano, Fall 2004

The Creative Workshop and how it affected my life. An excerpt from my musical diary:

II-V-I licks, Charlie Parker, Jimi Hendrix tossed out the window. In the Creative Workshop I myself began to dig a little deeper into my creative imagination; composing free of form, chords, and standard rules. If there was a place to break the rules, and an opportunity to do so, this was going to be it. Whether it was playing guitar with my feet, jamming with a painter, interpreting the leaves of autumn falling off the tree branches, the tools I left with have inspired me to play on a path less traveled.

Blaze McKenzie, Fall 2005

CreW has opened up avenues of expression that I had previously never explored. I left every class satisfied. It was a supportive environment where all ideas, regardless of idiomatic relevance, were accepted.

Adam Tressler, Fall 2005

For me, the most important aspect of the workshop was being in a comfortable environment, especially for trying out new ideas. The workshop definitely altered how I think about music; my approach to improvisation has changed. I was challenged to improvise in unfamiliar mediums, with sculptors and dancers.

Nico Alzetta, Fall 2006

The workshop techniques help me go to places that were inconceivable for me three months ago. It was the most fun course I've ever taken. The most important thing in music and art is to learn to think like a three-year old.

Braydon Nelson, Fall 2006

True outside of the box thinking.

Az Samad, Spring 2006

I found the Creative Workshop to be a challenging and inspiring class, constantly surprising me and helping me think in different ways. Workshop techniques have made their way into my composing and performance. Forgetting stylistic boundaries made me more open to embracing all musical influences from the past. In my case, the class made me go back to my more childlike approaches to music: what does that sound make, what are all the sounds I have?

Daniel Wright, Fall 2006

This is the only class worth waking up for at 8 a.m. on a Monday morning.

Josh Gerowitz, Spring 2007

I took the Creative Workshop with Jon Damian in the spring of 2007, which was during my last semester at Berklee College of Music. The class had a great impact on the way I thought about music and possible methods of creating it. The following summer I was hired to resurrect the music program at the California Medical Facility in Vacaville, California. CMF is a prison hospital which houses the largest population of AIDS patients anywhere in the United States. Most of my students were in prison for life, and a large portion of them were so heavily medicated that it was quite difficult for them to absorb the information I was trying to teach them. I struggled for a while trying to develop a program that would not only teach the inmates to become better musicians but would also teach them teamwork and community. I also had the more ambitious goal of demonstrating the power music has to transport, transcend, and heal in the way that all people who have been touched by music are familiar with.

Somewhere during the middle of my time at CMF I began running my own version of the Creative Workshop, and I immediately noticed positive and encouraging results. At first it was difficult for everyone to drop their guard and fully enter into the mind-set that is necessary to perform and experience this type of material. Once that was accomplished, the mood and atmosphere of the classroom changed. One of the highlights of this experience was rehearsing and performing with the inmates a piece I had written for Jon Damian's Creative Workshop called "Spider Webs." The classes took place in what was a locked medical examination room where I was alone with 15 or so inmates, and during this particular instance the music just started really happening; we were all in the moment, and no one was projecting their self-doubt or hesitation into the environment. All of a sudden, I felt as if the bright fluorescent lights reflecting off the linoleum floor was the only thing that was holding us back. So I switched off the lights, and we finished performing the piece in absolute darkness. Only upon conclusion of the piece did I realize that what I had done was incredibly unsafe, and possibly irresponsible. When I turned the lights back on we all discussed what had transpired, and one of my students told me that this was the first time he had traveled outside of the prison walls in years.

It is a real testament to Professor Damian's musicianship and technique that even after I moved across the country and entered a new phase of my life, the lessons I learned from working with him are still developing. I have never had an experience in which I felt better about something I have been a part of, and I am honored to be able to share the knowledge I gained during my time working with Jon Damian with my students, colleagues, and friends.

Graham Lambert, Spring 2007

Close your eyes, and play.

Pavel Rivera, Spring 2007

The Creative Workshop was an experience that led me to seek unusual sources of inspiration for my compositions and productions. For instance, sometimes when I'm on the train, I will get ideas from all the noises and cool sounds it makes. Or maybe I'll record the noise that an old printer makes when it prints, and then sample it to make a cymbal groove for an electronic beat. The workshop made me realize how wide a range of musical resources we have. The workshop and the friends I made definitely made an impact in my life!

Dan Gianaris, Spring 2011

The Creative Workshop Ensemble was so richly inspiring for me musically that it is challenging to single out the concepts and ideas that most benefited me. There were two concepts that left the biggest impact on me. They both illustrated how much can be done with a limited amount of material. In one exercise a standard tune was chosen; "Take the A Train" was my choice. We literally chopped the phrases of the melody into fragments and rearranged them. The result was a completely new tune, a musical collage reflecting Duke's classic, but with a character all its own. For the next concept we took a very simple melody—I chose "Happy Birthday"—and attempted to disguise it by keeping the same order of notes, and only changing the notes' rhythms and directions well enough to fool our classmates. This is harder than it sounds, because to you as a writer, it's nearly impossible to lose the original tune. To the listener, on the other hand, it's very hard to pick up. Both of these ideas are very useful in improvisation and composition. I share both of these ideas with my students.

The Creative Workshop Ensemble also challenged my idea of what a composition is. We would play pieces based on stories, or drawings, or based on verbal directions given by our fellow workshop members. These pieces would be very successful, creating unique musical environments unachievable with standard notation. Another one of my favorite workshop concepts was based on Béla Bartók's *Concerto for Orchestra*. First we listened to the opening three minutes of the concerto's introduction and took notes in real time about what was happening in the music. This quick "transcription" led itself to beautiful "comprovisations" by workshop members.

David Lee, Spring and Fall 2011

For most seekers, and students, the world of art and music is a place of wonder and beauty. It's a world accessible through any number of atlases, documentaries, tourists' books, or, if they're lucky, a tour guide. Jon lives in this world. The Creative Workshop is an invitation to not only visit this world, but to be immersed in it—speaking, seeing, hearing, choosing, thinking, and living as a creative resident. The Workshop is a place to find creative peers, emerging talented fellow students, and spirit guides from history. Through example, guidance, inspiration, history, and insightful assignment, each student comes to own a piece of this world.

Jon's Creative Workshop was a singular experience in my time at Berklee (a singular experience I returned to several times). It was through the Workshop that I found an awareness that art is the articulation of life's expression. Today I'm a native speaker.

Jernej Bervar, Spring 2012

Being part of the Creative Workshop was like being in a mad scientist's lab. We discovered things beyond my imagination, that inspire my music to this day. Want to be a better and more creative musician? Jon Damian's methods are at the leading edge of music education today.

JON: A final thank you, CreW, for your creative spirits. I enjoyed our work together and learned some wonderful things from you. I have the raw recording of our work, which I will mix and get to you electronically.

CHAPTER 15
THE FOLDER CHAPTER

*After silence, that which comes nearest to expressing
the inexpressible is music.*
—Aldous Huxley

Readers, here is your workshop folder, which includes the handouts given during the semester.

THE CREATIVE WORKSHOP ENSEMBLE FLYER
WELCOME TO THE CREATIVE WORKSHOP ENSEMBLE (CREW)

The Creative Workshop Ensemble is one of my favorite creative experiences, and I have been enjoying its rewards and challenges since I originally conceived of the workshop as an ensemble for improvisational and compositional explorations in all art media. In 1978 I first offered the Creative Workshop as a performance experience at Berklee College of Music.

As a member of the Creative Workshop Ensemble, affectionately and acronymically referred to as CreW, you follow in the path of many admirable members. I often receive correspondence from former workshop members, filled with wonderful memories of their workshop experience. Every workshop member has a unique personality, and these traits combine to make each workshop a special, challenging experience. Ideally, members function as a team, helping to fully realize each of their creative ideas through discussion and execution of these ideas. As workshop members, let us think of ourselves as *polyartists*, artists in *all* media, as sound *and* visual artists, painters, sculptors, dancers, actors, authors, parents, culinary artists, and many more, for they are all connected and nourished by our creative spirit.

In the workshop, infinite sources are used for inspiration for ideas. Through this process, workshop members eventually realize the ability to draw upon anything in the universe as a potential foundation from which to build creative works as well as discovering their innate creative genius.

An important workshop goal is to develop a creative communication system, beginning with each workshop member finding an idea and developing the member's ability to express and implement this idea with the rest of the workshop. The successful group performance of these ideas then depends on each player's *group* communication, listening, and watching skills, in order for each to be an integral part of the whole. A total openness to fellow workshop members' new ideas inspires the teamwork that makes this workshop what it is, an open forum. Think of me as a workshop member, not only as a teacher. I will also bring in and share my own works with you.

Your ideas may originally be offered and finally executed in any *combination* of formats, and in any art medium you think will be effective in expressing yourself. Remember, the world is your palette and your medium. Let us think of ourselves as artists in all media—whether good or bad is meaningless for our purposes

As a final project, starting in week 12, we will create a recording of some of our work. This is an important documentation of our accomplishments, and a wonderful way for you to sit back and enjoy your very unique workshop in action.

Important things to *always* have with you each week.

Your fearlessness

Your imagination

Your instrument(s)

Your folder for the Creative Workshop Ensemble

Manuscript paper

A pencil

A sketchpad

Your love for one of your greatest gifts, your creative spirit

Thank you for becoming a part of the Creative Workshop Ensemble Family.

CReW Hand Signals

Readers: Adjust these hand signals as needed for your workshop's medium. For example, in a creative dance workshop, replace "play" with "dance." This is just a start. You can devise your own hand language.

BASIC START AND STOP PLAYING INDICATIONS

Start to play — A palm up and backward wave

Stop playing — A straightened finger(s) directed at player(s), and then making a horizontal slicing motion across neck!

REPEATING (LOOPING) INDICATIONS

Loop or repeat idea presently being played — Finger(s) pointed and twirling in a player's (or players') direction.

DYNAMIC INDICATIONS

Indicated player(s) become louder — Flattened palm up, rising vertically

Indicated player(s) become softer — Flattened palm down, descending vertically

Entire ensemble becomes louder — Both flattened palms up, rising vertically

Entire ensemble becomes softer — Both flattened palms down, descending vertically

SINGING INDICATIONS

Sing a *sustained* tone until you are out of breath or cut off — An extended index finger pointing at your open mouth

Sing actively until cue to cut — An extended index finger tapping at your open mouth

TONALITY INDICATIONS

Actual cue cards with tonality and quality of tonality written on them may be useful, but I find them to be cumbersome. For simplification, I use fingers to cue tonality and quality of tonality. I have found the finger language I present here to work well after some coaching with the ensemble.

INDICATING MAJOR TONALITY AND RELATED MODES

A specific major key — Key signature is indicated by the number of fingers of hand(s) held in an upward manner (number of sharps), or downward manner (number of flats).

A specific minor key — The previous major key signature indication followed by a thumbs down.

"The Village"

Readers, here is Bruno's final version of "The Village." He enlarged the font size so that everyone can step back from their stands and do some singing and dancing, and still see the indications.

The Village
Each of you is in a family in a village full of family sounds and energy.

Silently conceive of a repetitive, short, simple, groovy song, and a dance.

On the director's cue, everyone begin to actually sing and dance, and maintain your groove no matter what is happening around you. We want a rich effect here.

The director will then give hand signal cues for folks to sing louder or softer so we can enjoy taking a peek into each player's "home groove."

The director will also cue for the group to sing a long tone until you are out of breath, or to sing percussive sounds.

For the last section, the director will give extraction cues in which you extract just a little of your song and dance groove until gradually you are left with silence and stillness.

The director will then give a cue for everyone to sing a final long tone of their choice, which will naturally bring the piece to a final close.
FINE

"THE DEMOCRATIC CHORALE"

Here is the workshop's final version of "The Democratic Chorale," a nice-sounding series of democratic harmonies that can be used as is or as an accompaniment for an improviser or a composed melodic line. I am always searching for other democreative possibilities.

The Democratic Chorale

All structures democratically decided

Fig. 15.1. "The Democratic Chorale"

MASTY'S "DOMINOES STUDY #1"

Masty's "Dominoes Study #1" is for woodwind quartet. This is also a pretty piece for two guitars. She gives us some interesting structural details back in chapter 13 that got old Chester riled up.

Fig. 15.2. Masty's "Dominoes Study #1"

THE SIGHT-READING BIBLIOGRAPHY

Here is a bibliography that addresses the study of sight-reading, a valuable tool in our music study and careers. The titles are in three categories: books that develop reading skills as performers, books that develop reading skills as observers, and books that develop your body as a reading instrument. There are important observations to be made by studying music literacy from these three vantage points.

YOU AS PERFORMER

Well-composed and well-marked duet materials are valuable for study. You can study one part of the duet and record it, and then work up the other part of the duet. When playing and hearing both parts together, you develop an ensemble ability, creating a musical interplay and group consciousness. The Béla Bartók *44 Violin Duets* are also great springboards for improvisation.

Bartók, Béla. *44 Violin Duets Vols. I & II.* New York: Boosey and Hawkes, 1939.
Koehler, Ernesto. *40 Progressive Duets Opus 55.* New York: Carl Fischer, 1947.
Leavitt, William G. *Melodic Rhythms.* Boston: Berklee Press, 2000.
Nelson, Oliver. *Patterns for Improvisation.* Los Angeles: Noslen Press, 1966.
Voisin, Roger. *Develop Sight-Reading Vols. I & II.* New York: Charles Colin, 1972.

YOU AS OBSERVER

Following along with a music score while listening to the piece is inspirational in the study of reading music, not unlike watching a sport being played at a professional level. You will gain an appreciation for the art of reading. The Norton Scores volumes are a series of books that contain many scores. The recordings of many of these scores can be found in most major library networks. Here is just one of the Norton Scores volumes.

Kamien, Roger. *The Norton Scores: An Anthology for Listening.* New York: W. W. Norton & Co., 1990.

YOU AS INSTRUMENT

As we have been exploring throughout *Fresh Music,* making ourselves instruments through singing and dancing enables us to become the music. These books help to develop our inner sight-reading abilities with our external and internal voices.

Bona, Pasquale. *Rhythmic Articulation.* New York: Calmus, 1989.
Prosser, Steve. *Intervallic Ear Training for Musicians.* Boston: Sol Ra Press, 1990.

IN CLOSING AND A THANK YOU

> *Our function as artists is to show the rest of the*
> *world that infinity still exists.* —Naimad Noj

This book would not be possible without all the wonderful Creative Workshop Ensemble members—including you, dear readers—who are now contributing their inspirations to the workshop's consciousness. Thank you for your attention, and for reading *Fresh Music: Explorations with the Creative Workshop Ensemble for Musicians, Artists, and Teachers*. I thank you, my fellow polyartists in all media. I hope to someday see, and hear, and feel, and smell, and taste your artistic creations. Send them to me.

Peace and Love,

jon

Jon Damian

Berklee College of Music
1140 Boylston St.
Boston, MA 02215
(617) 747-8152

jdamian@berklee.edu
jondamian.com

BIBLIOGRAPHY

Barlow, Harold, and Sam Morgenstern. *A Dictionary of Musical Themes*. New York: Crown Publishers, 1948.

Benade, Arthur. *Horns, Strings, and Harmony*. New York: Dover Press, 1992.

Buonopane, Marguerite. *The North End Union Italian Cookbook*. Guilford, CT: Globe Pequot Press, 1987.

Cage, John. *Notations*. New York: Something Else Press, 1996.

Cameron, Julia. *The Artist's Way*. New York: Jeremy P. Tarcher/Putnam, 2006.

Challoner, Jack. *The 1001 Inventions That Changed the World*. New York: Barron's Educational Series, 2009.

Cohan, Robert. *The Dance Workshop*. New York: Simon & Schuster, 1986.

Damian, Jon. *The Guitarist's Guide to Composing and Improvising*. Boston: Berklee Press, 2001.

_____. *The Chord Factory: Build Your Own Chord Dictionary*. Boston: Berklee Press, 2007.

Doczi, Gyorgy. *The Power of Limits: Proportional Harmonies in Nature, Art, and Architecture*. Boston: Shambala Press, 2005.

Elliot, Lang. *Music of the Birds*. Boston: Houghton Mifflin, 1999.

Gallwey, W. Timothy, and Barry Green. *The Inner Game of Music*. Garden City, NY: Doubleday, 1986.

Gold, Robert S. *A Jazz Lexicon*. New York: Alfred A. Knopf, 1964.

Gooders, John. *The Great Book of Birds*. New York: The Dial Press, 1975.

Minton, Sandra Cerny. *Choreography*. Champaign, IL: Human Kinetics, 2007.

The New Harvard Dictionary of Music. Cambridge, MA: Belknap Press, 1986.

Partch, Harry. *Genesis of a Music*. Cambridge, MA: Da Capo Press, 1974.

Passolli, Robert. *A Book on the Open Theatre*. New York: Macmillan, 1970.

Persichetti, Vincent. *Twentieth-Century Harmony*. New York: W.W. Norton & Co., 1961.

Schafer, R. Murray. *Creative Music Education*. New York: Schirmer Books, 1976.

Slonimsky, Nicolas. *Thesaurus of Scales and Melodic Patterns*. 1st. ed. New York: Schirmer Trade Books, 1975.

Whelan, Jeremy. *The ABC's of Acting*. West Linn, OR: Grey Heron Books, 1991.

Poems "hybridized" in Chapter 2, "Poetical Variations" exercise, p. 27–28.

Joyce Kilmer, "Trees," *Modern American Poetry* (New York: Harcourt, Brace and Howe, 1919); Bartleby.com, 1999.

A. E. Housman, "Loveliest of Trees," *A Shropshire Lad* (London: K. Paul, Trench, Treubner, 1896).

Percy Bysshe Shelley, "To a Skylark," *The Complete Poetical Works of Percy Bysshe Shelley, Centenery Edition in Four Volumes,* vol. 3 (Boston: Houghton Mifflin and Company, 1982), p. 270.

Edith Thomas, "The Vesper Sparrow," *In Sunshine Land* (Boston: Houghton Mifflin Company, 1894), p. 47.

Samuel Taylor Coleridge, "Kubla Khan," *The Complete Poems of Samuel Taylor Coleridge*, ed. William Keach (New York: Penguin Books, 2004).

CPSIA information can be obtained at www.ICGtesting.com
Printed in the USA
BVOW08s1320200615

404850BV00001B/1/P